Fateful Months

FATEFUL MONTHS

Essays on the Emergence
of the Final Solution

Christopher R. Browning

HM

HOLMES & MEIER
New York   London

First published in the United States of America 1985 by
Holmes & Meier Publishers, Inc.
30 Irving Place
New York, N.Y. 10003

Great Britain:
Holmes & Meier Publishers, Ltd.
Unit 5   Greenwich Industrial Estate
345 Woolwich Road   Charlton, London SE7

Book design by Stephanie Greco

Library of Congress Cataloging in Publication Data

Browning, Christopher R.
   Fateful months: Essays on the emergence of the final
solution.

   Includes index.
   1. Holocaust, Jewish (1939–1945)—Yugoslavia—Serbia.
2. Jews—Yugoslavia—Serbia—Persecutions.   3. Serbia—
Ethnic relations.   I. Title.
DS135.Y82S493   1985   940.51'15'0392404971   84-8089
ISBN 0-8419-0967-9

Manufactured in the United States of America

For Jennifer, Kathryn, and Anne

Contents

Acknowledgments

This book could not have been written without the help of many people and institutions. Above all, the generous support of the Alexander von Humboldt Foundation and a sabbatical leave from Pacific Lutheran University made possible a year of indispensable archival research in Europe.

The staffs of the Bundesarchiv Koblenz, the Politisches Archiv des Auswärtigen Amtes in Bonn, the Jevrejski Istorijski Muzej (Jewish History Museum) in Belgrade, and the Institut für Zeitgeschichte in Munich ably assisted my research at their respective institutions. Leitender Oberstaatsanwalt Dr. Adalbert Rückerl and Herr Krantz of the Zentrale Stelle der Landesjustizverwaltungen, Mr. Daniel Simon and Herr Pix of the Berlin Document Center, Lieutenant Colonel General Fabian Trgo and Lieutenant Colonel Antun Miletič of the Vojno Istorijski Institut in Belgrade, Herr Meyer of the Bundesarchiv-Militärarchiv Freiburg and Archivoberinspektorin Bauerschäfer of the Staatsarchiv Nürnberg deserve special mention.

My research was heavily dependent upon access to German court records. Staatsanwalt Landgraf in Hannover, Staatsanwalt Dr. Gollrad in Stuttgart, Oberstaatsanwalt Tschepke in Kassel, Staatsanwalt Lang in Köln, Leitender Oberstaatsanwalt Dr. Wetterich in Konstanz, and Oberstaatsanwalt Schacht in Dortmund gave the necessary permission and facilitated my research in the relevant court records under their jurisdictions.

Professor Dr. Hans Mommsen of the Ruhr-Universität Bochum served as my Humboldt Foundation sponsor and supported my research endeavors in many ways. Leitender Oberstaatsanwalt Pollig in Bonn gave very helpful advice. Colonel Fred Seamon, Cynthia Efird, and Ruth Kurzbauer of the American Embassy in Belgrade provided essential aid in gaining access to Yugoslav archives. Dr. Menachem Shelah generously shared his considerable expertise on the Holocaust in Serbia. My colleagues, Dr. Philip Nordquist and Dr. Mordechai Rozanski, read substantial portions of the manuscript, which benefited from their suggestions. Stimulating conversations with Dr. Raul Hilberg and Dr. Michael Marrus helped to refine some of the views I have attempted to express. None of the above, of course, are responsible for any shortcomings in the final product.

Dr. François Furet of the École des Hautes Études en Sciences Sociales in Paris, Dr. Klaus Maier of *Militärgeschichtliche Mitteilungen,* and Dr. Livia Rothkirchen of *Yad Vashem Studies* kindly granted permission to include materials (Chapters 1, 2, and 4 respectively) originally published under their auspices.

The late Dr. Nada Pavličev and Sergei Pavličev provided the most gracious hospitality in Yugoslavia. Olga Browning translated several important documents from Serbo-Croatian. Finally, my wife and daughters tolerated one of the most inconvenient research itineraries imaginable and, from Bonn to Belgrade, sustained my efforts with their patient good will and loving support.

Fateful Months

Introduction

In May 1940 the itinerant euthanasia squad known as *Sonderkommando* Lange traveled from its headquarters in Posen to the transit camp at Soldau in East Prussia, where, between May 21 and June 6, it murdered 1,558 mental patients culled from nearby asylums. In September 1940, SS-*Oberscharführer* (Sergeant) Seith, a driver from the Gestapo and a member of *Sonderkommando* Lange, wrote to his former "host," the Higher SS and Police Leader in Königsberg:

> After many difficulties your "personal souvenir from East Prussia," the little amber box with the dedication of the Gauleiter, has finally reached me. My joy over this is very great, because aside from the unforgettable social evening and farewell party in Soldau, this is the sole recognition of our action, and you experienced only a fraction of that.
> The action would never have taken place, if it were to have been done by us for personal gain, and thus I was put to a hard test in Posen when I asked for 30 days (we get 72 per year) and they threatened to let me go if I remained adamant on claiming my vacation.
> You will understand, that in these circumstances your gift gives me double the pleasure because of its thoughtfulness.
> My thanks shall be that also in the future I will do more than my duty.[1]

On July 16, 1941, SS-*Sturmbannführer* Rolf Heinz Höppner in Posen wrote to "dear comrade Eichmann," summarizing the discussion of a series of local conferences on "the solution of the Jewish question in the Warthegau." After discussing the possibility of concentrating all Warthegau Jews in a huge labor camp, thus requiring fewer guards and lessening the chance of epidemic then threatening the ghettos, the conference participants considered two further proposals.

> There exists this winter the danger that all the Jews can no longer be fed. It should be seriously considered if it would not be the most humane solu-

tion to dispose of the Jews, insofar as they are not capable of work, through a quick-acting agent. In any case it would be more pleasant than to let them starve.

In addition the proposal was made to sterilize all the female Jews in this camp from whom children could still be expected, so that with this generation the Jewish problem is in fact completely solved.

Asking for Eichmann's opinion, Höppner concluded, "These things sound somewhat fantastic but are in my opinion definitely feasible."[2]

We do not know if Sergeant Seith, filled with great joy over his souvenir of East Prussia, continued to forego his vacation for the privilege of remaining in Lange's murder squad and thus had the chance once again to do "more than his duty" when that *Sonderkommando* opened the first Nazi death camp at Chelmno in the Warthegau on December 8, 1941. Furthermore, we do not know if the "somewhat fantastic" proposal of the SS-officers in Posen for disposing of Jews "through a quick-acting agent" as the "most humane solution" played any direct role in the founding of that first camp at Chelmno.[3] Such rare documents, however, give the historian a brief glimpse into the minds of the lower echelon perpetrators on the eve of the Final Solution. Such a glimpse is important to correct the temptation toward an overly Hitlerocentric interpretation, one that focuses exclusively on the intentions and decisions of Hitler at the top while ignoring the attitudes and behavior of those at the bottom.

Certainly the intentions and decisions of Hitler were vitally important, and the controversy over the nature of Hitler's role in the Final Solution has been a justly prominent topic in Holocaust studies in recent years. My own contribution to that debate follows in the next chapter. But regardless of the stance one takes on this question—whether Hitler was the instigator and inciter of a radicalizing Nazi Jewish policy but unaware of precisely where it would lead until 1941, or whether he decided then that the time was ripe to implement his long-held extermination plan—one fact is undisputable: Hitler alone did not murder the European Jews. Even if Hitler had long intended to murder the Jews and merely awaited the opportune moment, such a decision for implementing the Final Solution would not have been forthcoming without his judgment that many people were eagerly prepared to take the initiative in solving the multitude of problems a mass-murder program posed, that many more were prepared to participate in such a program as long as their participation could be made part of an unthinking routine or job, and that even more were prepared passively to acquiesce in or shut their eyes to what their government was doing.

That a solution of mass murder could be deemed practicable and the participation and acquiescence of wide circles of German society could be counted upon by the upper echelons of the Nazi regime are virtually incomprehensible if not viewed in a broader historical context. The distressing fact is that mass killing as state policy had already become fairly widespread by 1941. The murder of Hitler's opponents, mostly Communists and Socialists but also Roehm and the SA-leadership, in the first years of the dictatorship, followed by intensifying anti-Jewish measures and the internment in concentration camps of so-called "asocials" such as homosexuals, was not so much a cause for alarm as a source of reassurance to all too many Germans that the Nazis were taking strong steps to remove the sources of unrest, subversion, disintegration, corruption, and moral decay from German society. In January 1939 Hitler announced to the Reichstag his prophecy that if war came, it would result in the destruction of the Jews in Europe. On August 22, 1939, he allegedly announced to his generals:

> Genghis Khan had millions of women and children killed by his own will and with a gay heart. History sees in him only a great state builder. What weak Western civilization thinks about me does not matter. . . . I have sent to the East my "Death's Head Units" with the order to kill without mercy all men, women, and children of the Polish race or language. Only in such a way will we win the vital space that we need. Who still talks nowadays of the extermination of the Armenians?[4]

While the threats totally to destroy both Jews and Poles were not carried out immediately following the outbreak of war, which should caution the historian from taking such statements by Hitler as literal orders or explicit decisions, the fact remains that many Polish Jews were killed in random massacres and the Polish intelligentsia was systematically executed. The practice of mass murder was growing, and not only in the occupied territories but in Germany as well. Following the invasion of Poland Hitler ordered the commencement of the so-called euthanasia program, which over the next two years murdered at least seventy thousand Germans who were deemed "unworthy of life." The victims were selected from Germany's asylums and hospitals by medical personnel, transferred through one or more intermediate stops (the Nazis in effect "laundered" people the way white-collar criminals "launder" money), and finally sent to the euthanasia institutes and murdered in gas chambers with carbon monoxide. Thus Germans were the first gassing victims, which should also caution historians from taking as an open declaration of Hitler's future intentions his statement in *Mein Kampf* lamenting that twelve thousand to fifteen thousand Jews had not been gassed during the First World War.

Through all this the Nazi regime enjoyed the support and cooperation of the older elites in German society, even if the latter did not yet participate directly in the mass-murder programs. The Foreign Office defended the Nazi regime and its policies, including the persecution of the Jews, against foreign criticism. The Interior Ministry authored much anti-Jewish legislation. The Economics Ministry helped carry out the confiscation of Jewish property.[5] The army rearmed, swore personal loyalty to Hitler, became his instrument of military expansion, and—apart from a few individual officers—accommodated itself to the systematic violation of international law. Moreover, the army demonstrated its acceptance of the Nazi image of the Jew as the enemy when it excluded Jews from the compulsory military service reintroduced in March 1935 and when the military administration in occupied territories introduced and enforced various anti-Jewish measures.[6]

In the wake of the spectacular victory in the west in 1940, there fell by the wayside any lingering reticence on the part of the German officer corps and ministerial bureaucracy, once the proud and dominant elites in Germany society, to participate in not only the military and political but now also the mass-murder programs of the Nazis. Planning for Operation Barbarossa entailed both the mass murder of Russian Jews and the widespread killing and starvation of millions of other Russians. By the spring of 1942, when the Final Solution in Europe was just getting underway, some two million Russian prisoners of war in the merciless custody of the German army had already died of starvation, illness, exposure, or execution.[7] This significantly exceeded the number of Jews who had already perished before the SS firing squads or in the starving, disease-ridden ghettos in Poland and Russia. In short, the Final Solution did not emerge in a political vacuum but rather was the culminating development of a political system in which mass murder had become accepted practice.

The degree to which the Final Solution was compatible with the temper of the times can be seen in the proposal of the SS-officers of Posen to kill Jews who could not work and sterilize the surviving females, "so that with this generation the Jewish problem is in fact completely solved." Others did not just propose but acted; they found their way to the mass murder of Jews on their own, even before the Final Solution was underway. One example is the Wehrmacht execution of the male Jews in Serbia, which is discussed in detail in Chapter 2.

Even with such growing acclimatization to the policy of mass murder and Hitler's decision to extend it to the European Jews, the means to accomplish this were not self-evident. If mass murder was not new, the sheer magnitude and intended thoroughness of the Final Solution were unprecedented. The *Einsatzgruppen* campaign had already demonstrated, even for Russia, the inadequacy of firing-squad execution in terms of the psychological burden on the executioners, the lack of secrecy, and the difficulty of coping with the huge numbers of victims. Methods that were more detached, more efficient, and less visible had to be developed; the death camp had to be conceived, approved, constructed, and, along with the supporting deportation apparatus, put into operation—a process that lasted, I would argue, from the late summer of 1941 to the spring of 1942. In the meantime the Nazis struggled to make do with the latest technological means already at their disposal—the gas van. The development and production of the gas van is studied in Chapter 3. A case study of its deployment and use in the interim mini-death camp of Semlin outside Belgrade is presented in Chapter 4. With such stopgap measures the Germans were able to get the Final Solution underway, even before the death camps equipped with stationary gas chambers were ready.

Careful study of events in late 1941 and early 1942 is important in order to understand how the Germans took the first steps in the Final Solution at the local level. Such study of events at the local level also enriches our understanding of the decision-making process at the center. A variety of interpretation has flourished concerning Hitler's role in the decision for the Final Solution because no key document has been found that reveals precisely how and when, or even if, Hitler made such a decision and passed it on to Göring, Himmler, and Heydrich. The search for a single decisive and incriminating document, a "smoking pistol," has not been successful and is in all likelihood futile, for such a document probably never existed. The search for evidence must of necessity be more indirect. One must shift away from an exclusively Hitlerocentric focus and look much more carefully at what the middle- and lower-echelon Germans of the emerging "machinery of destruction" were doing. Once the historian has a better understanding of what was happening in the field and when the future perpetrators of the Final Solution first knew what they were about, he can then draw certain conclusions or at least hazard more informed speculation about what had taken place at the center of the Nazi regime. All the essays in this collection are an attempt to look at various aspects of Nazi Jewish policy in the fall of 1941 and spring of 1942 in this light. They study new evidence concerning hitherto relatively unexamined incidents that occurred during this fateful transition period in Nazi Jewish policy and draw conclusions about what this new evidence reveals as to how that fateful transition took place. They attempt to shed light on the emergence of the Final Solution by looking both from the top down and from the bottom up.

1

The Decision Concerning
the Final Solution

The decision concerning the Final Solution has been the subject of a wide variety of historical interpretation. The major differences emerge over two related questions: first, the nature of the decision-making process, with particular focus on the role of Hitler and his ideology; and second, the timing of the decision. Such a variety of interpretation warns us, as Martin Broszat has correctly pointed out, that any thesis concerning the origins of the Final Solution is a matter of probability, not certainty.[1] In this light I present the following thesis. The intention of systematically murdering the European Jews was not fixed in Hitler's mind before the war, but crystallized in 1941 after previous solutions proved unworkable and the imminent attack upon Russia raised the prospect of yet another vast increase in the number of Jews within the growing German empire. The Final Solution emerged out of a series of decisions taken that year. In the spring Hitler ordered preparations for the murder of the Russian Jews who would fall into German hands during the coming invasion. That summer, confident of military victory, Hitler instigated the preparation of a plan to extend the killing process to European Jews. In October, although military expectations had not been realized, Hitler approved the rough outline of that plan, involving deportation to killing centers using poison gas. While I wish to give special attention to the arguments and evidence concerning the course of events in the summer and fall of 1941, which I consider so crucial, let us first briefly review the historiography of the issue.

In recent years interpretations of National Socialism have increasingly polarized between two groups aptly designated by Tim Mason as the "intentionalists" and the "functionalists."[2] The former explain the course of Nazi Germany in terms of Hitler's intentions derived from a coherent and consistent ideology and implemented through an all-powerful totalitarian dictatorship; the latter emphasize the anarchical nature of the Nazi state, its internal competition, and the chaotic decision-making process that resulted in continuous improvisation and radicalization. The "intentionalists" do not deny the polycratic nature of the Nazi state, but portray it as the conscious product of Hitler's Machiavellian cunning, cleverly manipulated to realize his fixed intentions. The "functionalists" do not deny that Hitler played a central role but see this role as a mobilizing and integrating agent. Thus for them, Hitler's limitless hatred of the Jews and his aggressive and destructive impulses gave an overarching unity of purpose and direction to the chaotic Nazi state but only at the cost of constant radicalization culminating in a *Vernichtungskrieg* in the east, genocide of the European Jews, and ultimately overwhelming defeat.[3]

These two modes of historical explanation are useful in analyzing the vastly differing interpretations concerning German Jewish policy in general and the decision for the Final Solution in particular. At one extreme the ultraintentionalist Lucy Dawidowicz has argued that as early as 1919 Hitler decided to exterminate the European Jews. Moreover, he knew when the murderous plan would be implemented. The Second World War was to be both the means and the occasion intended by Hitler to carry out his premeditated, genocidal "war against the Jews." While Hitler awaited the predetermined moment to carry out his "grand design," however, he tolerated a meaningless and irrelevant pluralism in Jewish policy in the lower echelons of the state and party.[4]

If Dawidowicz emphasized the element of Hitler's premeditation and "grand design," the German intentionalist historians writing in the 1960's—Helmut Krausnick, Andreas Hillgruber, Eberhard Jäckel, and Karl Dietrich Bracher—had held a considerably less conspiratorial view that stressed the early crystallization of Hitler's murderous intentions towards the Jews and the ensuing "continuity" of Nazi Jewish policy that culminated in the Final Solution. In their view Hitler's anti-Semitism was a key element of his *Weltanschauung;* his racial and territorial goals—mass murder of the Jews and the achievement of *Lebensraum* in the east—were inextricably bound together in a henceforth firmly fixed set of long-range priorities or "unalterable" program. The continuity between Hitler's ideas in the 1920's and Nazi policies in the 1940's was a clear indication of the dominant position Hitler held in the Third Reich and the primacy of the ideological factor in understanding his actions. There may have been no precise "blueprint" or "master plan" by which Nazi Jewish policy unfolded, but there was consciousness and calculation; Hitler knew what he wanted and exploited the available opportunities ultimately to realize his long-range goals. The Final Solution was, in Bracher's words, "merely a matter of time and opportunity." From this perspective the Nazi persecution of the Jews in the 1930s was a steady, preparatory crescendo restrained only by tactical considerations from reaching the murderous climax intimated by many Hitler statements. The emigration schemes between 1938 and 1940, from Rublee to Madagascar, were not serious alternatives. The attack on Russia to attain *Lebensraum* was inherently connected—both emotionally and logically—to the other principal ideological goal of Hitler's program, the extermination of the Jews. Thus Hitler's decision finally to implement the Final Solution was taken during the preparations for that attack—sometime between the summer of 1940 and the spring of 1941.[5] Subsequent advocates of the intentionalist view have been Gerald Fleming, who has asserted a "dead-straight path" *(schnurrgerade Weg)* from Hitler's prewar anti-Semitism in Vienna to the Final Solution, and the more eclectic Sarah Gordon, who has postulated an "abstract decision" for extermination sometime between 1924 and 1936 and certainly no later than 1939.[6]

The contrasting functionalist interpretation appeared in the early 1970's. Karl Schleunes and Uwe Dietrich Adam challenged the idea that Nazi Jewish policy could be understood in terms of a calculated plan aimed at achieving the premeditated goal of mass murder. Dissecting the "twisted road" that Nazi Jewish policy followed in the 1930s, they concluded that no uniform Nazi Jewish policy existed. Rather, various agencies and organizations within the party and state pursued different and often conflicting Jewish policies. Because Hitler's interventions were in fact quite infrequent and ambiguous, the competitors were left to fight it out in a Darwinian power struggle. Only the SS, which gradually entered the fray after 1935, had a clear concept in mind of a "final solution" to the Jewish question—a totally *judenrein* Germany through systematic emigration. In 1938–1939 the SS triumphed over its rivals and took the leading role in shaping Nazi Jewish policy: its various schemes for mass emigration and resettlement were "genuine." Only the failure of these schemes on the one hand and the ongoing commitment of the Nazis to solve the Jewish question on the other prepared the way for the last fatal step to mass murder in 1941. Thus the Final Solution was not a premeditated goal toward which Hitler and the Nazis consciously strived; rather it was the unplanned product of an evolutionary process in which Hitler and his ideology played a much less dominant role than in the interpretation of the intentionalists.[7]

Ironically, the closest thing to a definitive work on the Final Solution, Raul Hilberg's magnificent *The Destruction of the European Jews,* which first appeared in 1961 before the polarization between intentionalists and functionalists took place, remained strangely untouched by the controversy, seldom cited or invoked by either side. In part this was because Hilberg concentrated on the implementation rather than the genesis of the Final Solution. But in addition Hilberg's interpretation did not lend itself readily to use by either intentionalists or functionalists. In contrast to the former, he did not emphasize the personal role and ideology of Hitler. Instead Hilberg focused on the administrative structure of the Final Solution, composed of the four hierarchies of party, army, industry, and ministerial bureaucracy which were fused into a single "machinery of destruction." Denying the existence of a "master plan" or "basic blueprint," Hilberg concluded that the "German bureaucracy was so sensitive a mechanism that in the right climate it began to function almost by itself" and "did not have to be told what to do."[8] If Hilberg's non-Hitlerocentric view gave scant comfort to the intentionalists, other aspects of his interpretation disappointed the functionalists. The unity and cooperation, not the competitive disarray, of the German bureaucracy stood at center stage in Hilberg's book. In contrast to the "twisted road" of Schleunes and Adam, Hilberg had concluded: "With uncanny pathfinding ability, the German bureaucracy found the shortest road to the final goal." This was because the destruction process, in Hilberg's view, had an "inherent pattern" of its own—definition, confiscation, concentration, and destruction.[9] As the machinery of destruction gained momentum, the process developed systematically and logically out of its own inner necessity. In short, Hilberg denied that the Nazis were conscious of the final goal of mass murder, but he nonetheless emphasized a continuity stemming from the bureaucratic structure and the destruction process itself. If the key issue was continuity, Hilberg could be invoked by the intentionalists; if the key issues were a lack of consciousness of the final goal and a deemphasis of Hitler's personal role, Hilberg stood closer to the functionalists.

In addition to the controversy over the long-term issues of continuity, consciousness, and the role of Hitler in the evolution of Nazi Jewish policy, there has also been considerable difference of opinion over the nature and timing of the immediate decision-making process in 1941. The intentionalists in general held that Hitler's decision to implement the Final Solution dated from the preparations for the attack on Russia. Jäckel initially placed this more precisely in the summer of 1940, immediately following the fall of France.[10] Others chose the spring of 1941, with the formation of the *Einsatzgruppen*.[11] For the intentionalists, Hitler's decision to murder the Russian Jews also sealed the fate of the European Jews. In contrast, Raul Hilberg noted, "Basically, we are dealing with two of Hitler's decisions." The decision to create the *Einsatzgruppen* in the spring of 1941 provided for the mass murder of the Russian Jews, but it was only in the summer of 1941 that Hitler gave the order for the destruction of the European Jews.[12] Uwe Adam downplayed the significance of the formation of the *Einsatzgruppen* (a "gruesome replica" of events in Poland on a "novel scale") and placed the ultimate decision to murder the European Jews not in the summer but rather in the fall of 1941. This occurred sometime between September and November, when mass murder became the only "way out" of a situation in which Hitler had set deportations from Germany in motion but the stalled military campaign in Russia had not secured the land necessary for a "territorial solution."[13]

This was the state of the controversy when David Irving's book, *Hit-*

ler's War, appeared in 1977. According to Irving, Hitler not only did not know until the fall of 1943 of the Final Solution being carried out behind his back by his underlings, but had explicitly forbidden the mass murder of the Jews.[14] In response Martin Broszat, one of the "founding fathers" of the functionalist interpretation of National Socialism in the 1960s, wrote a lengthy critical review of Irving, in which he also stated his own thesis on the genesis of the Final Solution.[15] In Broszat's view Hitler made no ultimate decision and issued no comprehensive order for the Final Solution. Rather the destruction process evolved gradually out of a series of separate killing actions in late 1941 and early 1942. These local massacres were improvised responses to an impossible situation created by two factors: first, the ideological and political pressure for a *judenrein* Germany, exerted above all by Hitler; and second, the military failure on the eastern front that caused a lack of both rail transport and reception areas for the Jews who were to be uprooted. Once underway, the killing program gradually became institutionalized, and having proved itself logistically the simplest solution, grew finally into a comprehensive and distinctive program. In this view Hitler was a catalyst but not the decision maker.

It was in fact this stimulating and provocative "ultrafunctionalist" thesis of Broszat in response to Irving, more than the shoddy sensationalism of the Irving thesis itself, that triggered a vigorous and prolific academic debate. The present author, along with Kurt Pätzold, Wolfgang Scheffler, and now Eberhard Jäckel, argued that the Final Solution emerged from a series of decisions stretching from the spring to the fall of 1941.[16] Other viewpoints on both the beginning and endpoints of this process emerged simultaneously. First Christian Streit and then, in much greater detail, Alfred Streim challenged the notion that the formation of the *Einsatzgruppen* in the spring of 1941 was already tied to the decision to murder all the Russian Jews; in their view the decision for comprehensive murder, including women and children, came only in the summer.[17] Helmut Krausnick and Hans-Heinrich Wilhelm, in contrast, defended the more traditional viewpoint that the *Einsatzgruppen*'s murderous task was determined prior to the invasion of Russia.[18] At the other end of the year, both Sebastian Haffner and Shlomo Aronson, arguing within the context of Hitler's overall strategic vision, placed his decision to murder the European Jews only in late 1941. Haffner opted for December 1941, when the Russian counteroffensive dashed Hitler's hopes for a rapprochement with England following early German victory in the east. No longer having to remain an acceptable negotiating partner with the west, he switched priorities and now sought an irreversible racial victory over the Jews in place of the rapidly receding hopes for military victory.[19] Aronson opted for "late fall 1941" when American Lend-Lease to Russia (October 1) conclusively demonstrated that the extent of Jewish domination over the western democracies precluded any ultimate hope on Hitler's part for their acceptance of German hegemony in Europe. This not only removed the last diplomatic restraints to mass murder but added yet another spur to Hitler's fanatical desire to revenge himself on the Jews.[20] Finally, Hans Mommsen came vigorously to the defence of Broszat. Mommsen stated that "the path to the systematic policy of the Final Solution was taken only in late 1941." Though Hitler was the "ideological and political author" of the Final Solution, he did not set it in motion through a formal or even verbal order. Though a self-proclaimed structural historian, Mommsen ironically based his argument on a controversial psychological picture of Hitler. Mommsen portrayed Hitler as a "weak dictator" withdrawn from any real decision making in Jewish policy. He took refuge in propagandistic sloganeering and psychologically repressed the murderous reality that resulted from the actions of an ambitious Himmler and the inexorable SS bureaucrats who were determined to "transform the millennium into reality in the lifetime of the dictator" and made him the "slave of his own public prophecies" about the Jews.[21]

Why can such diversity of interpretation over the nature and timing of the decision for the Final Solution flourish? I would suggest two reasons. The first is one of definition. What is meant by a decision for the Final Solution? For the intentionalist, there were in fact two decisions. The first decision was the point at which the concept of the mass murder of the European Jews took form in Hitler's mind as a fixed goal—the point at which it became a part of his "unalterable program." The second decision was the point at which Hitler considered it opportune and possible to realize this goal. The former was determinative, the latter relatively incidental, for once the intention was fixed, Hitler had the power and cunning to realize it eventually. The functionalist makes no such clear distinction between the conceptualization and implementation of the Final Solution. Instead, in the functionalist view, the conception of systematic mass murder and the decision to implement it emerged simultaneously, products of a conjuncture of factors, of which Hitler's vicious anti-Semitism was but one. His ominous and threatening statements were not evidence of clearly held intentions but of an unquenchable hatred of the Jews that would spur a continuing radicalization of Jewish policy through a search and competition for final solutions to the Jewish question, until the "most final" of all—extermination—emerged. According to the functionalists, Hitler's ideological fixation assured that a Final Solution to the Jewish question would be sought, but not what specific form it would take.

A second reason for such diversity of interpretation is the lack of documentation. There are no written records of what took place among Hitler, Himmler, and Heydrich concerning the Final Solution, and none of them survived to testify after the war. Therefore, the decision-making process at the center must be reconstructed by the historian, who extrapolates from events, documents, and testimony originating outside the inner circle. Like the man in Plato's cave, he sees only the reflection and shadows, but not reality. This hazardous process of extrapolation and reconstruction inevitably invites. a wide variety of conclusions. Likewise, Hitler's thinking remains elusive. We cannot know precisely what was in his mind and again must reconstruct from recorded statements. This poses significant problems for the historian dealing with such a conscious political actor—one who could publicly threaten the Jews with destruction in 1939 and privately mention expulsion as late as January 1942.[22] The historian can avail himself of at least three approaches. First, he can through hindsight judge certain of Hitler's statements to be literal and dismiss the rest as duplicity, thus assuring a coherent ideology and a consistent but all too clever pattern of behavior on Hitler's part. Second, he can interpret many of Hitler's statements more figuratively, as "symbols of struggle" mobilizing and inciting his followers.[23] Finally, he can accept that Hitler experienced uncertainty and changes of mind and mood, and that contradictory statements are evidence of his own confusion.[24] Each of the above three approaches is valid at least in some cases, and thus the scope of possible interpretation is once again very wide.

Within the broad spectrum of interpretation, my thesis might be termed "moderate functionalist." I do not accept the intentionalists' view that the key decision—the conception of the Final Solution as a fixed goal—had already been taken long before the war and merely awaited the opportune moment for implementation. My position does not deny the significance of Hitler's anti-Semitism, only that the intention to murder the Jews had been consciously derived from it well in advance.

Concerning Hitler's anti-Semitism, historical consensus exists on the following: Psychologically, it was a deeply held obsession. Ideologically, it was the keystone of his *Weltanschauung*. Without his understanding of politics in terms of a Jewish-Bolshevik conspiracy and his understanding of history in terms of a Social-Darwinist struggle of races (in which the Jews played the most diabolical role), the whole edifice would collapse. Finally, Hitler gave expression to this anti-Semitism in violent threats and fantasies of mass murder.[25] Indeed, for a man whose Social Darwinism implied the final resolution of any conflict in terms of the survival of one adversary through the "destruction" of the other, and whose anti-Semitism was understood in terms of race, mass murder of the Jews was a "logical" deduction. Granted all this, the relationship between Hitler's anti-Semitism and the origin of the Final Solution still remains controversial.

Even if the Final Solution can be "logically" deduced from Hitler's *Weltanschauung*, it is improbable that Hitler made that deduction before 1941 and consciously pursued the systematic murder of the European Jews as a long-held goal. The assumption that Nazi Jewish policy was the premeditated and logical consequence of Hitler's anti-Semitism cannot be easily reconciled with his actual behavior in the years before 1941. For example, Hitler's view of the Jews as the "November criminals" who caused Germany's defeat in World War I was as fervently held as any of his anti-Jewish allegations. Indeed, the oft-cited passage from *Mein Kampf* lamenting that twelve or fifteen thousand Jews had not been gassed during the war makes far more sense in the context of the stab-in-the-back legend than as a prophecy or intimation of the Final Solution. The "logical" consequence of the thesis of the Jew as wartime traitor should have been a "preventive" massacre of German Jewry before the western offensive or at least before the attack on Russia.

In actual practice Nazi Jewish policy sought a *judenrein* Germany by facilitating and often coercing Jewish emigration. In order to reserve the limited emigration opportunities for German Jews, the Nazis opposed Jewish emigration from elsewhere on the continent. This policy continued until the fall of 1941, when the Nazis prohibited Jewish emigration from Germany and for the first time justified the blocking of Jewish emigration from other countries in terms of preventing their escape from the German grasp. The efforts of the Nazi Jewish experts to facilitate Jewish emigration both before and during the war, as well as their plans for massive expulsions (what the Nazis euphemistically called "resettlement" or *Umsiedlung*) were not merely tolerated but encouraged by Hitler.[26] It is difficult to reconcile the assumption of a long-held intention to murder the Jews of Europe with this behavior. If Hitler knew he was going to murder the Jews, then he was supporting a policy that "favored" German Jews over other European Jews and "rescued" from death many of those he held most responsible for Germany's earlier defeat.

It has been argued that Hitler was merely awaiting the opportune moment to realize his murderous intentions.[27] Not only does that not explain the pursuit of a contradictory policy of emigration in the meantime, it also does not explain the long delay. If Hitler was merely awaiting the outbreak of conflict to pursue his "war against the Jews," why were the millions of Polish Jews in his hands since the fall of 1939 granted a thirty-month "stay of execution"? They were subjected to sporadic massacre and murderous living conditions but not to systematic extermination until 1942. If Hitler could kill at least seventy thousand Germans through the euthanasia program between 1939 and 1941, why was it not "opportune" to murder several hundred thousand German Jews who constituted an "internal menace" in wartime? It certainly would have occasioned far less opposition than euthanasia. Why was this period not used to make preparations and plans for mass extermination, avoiding the clumsy improvisations of 1941? In short, the practice of Nazi Jewish policy until 1941 does not support the thesis of a long-held, fixed intention to murder the European Jews.

Hitler's anti-Semitism is more plausibly seen as the stimulant or spur to a continuous search for an increasingly radical solution to the Jewish question rather than as the source of a logically deduced and long-held "blueprint" for extermination. As the "satanic" figure behind all other problems, the Jew was for Hitler the ultimate problem and required an ultimate or final solution. Hitler's anti-Semitism thus constituted an ideological imperative which, given the competitive nature of the Nazi state, played a central role in the evolution of Nazi Jewish policy. The rival Nazi chieftains constantly sought to expand their private empires and vied for Hitler's favor through anticipating and pursuing Hitler's desires. In his function as arbiter, Hitler in turn sought to avoid totally antagonizing or alienating any of his close followers, even the most incompetent among them such as Rosenberg and Ribbentrop. Thus, when competing Nazis advocated conflicting policies, all plausibly justified in Nazi terminology, Hitler had great difficulty resolving differences. Paralysis and indecision were often the result. When, however, the competition was carried out at the expense of helpless third parties, such as Jews and populations of occupied territories, protected by no countervailing force, radicalization rather than paralysis followed. Hence it was the conjuncture of Hitler's anti-Semitic obsession, the anarchical and competitive nature of the Nazi state, the vulnerable status of the European Jews, and the war that resulted in the Final Solution.

By 1941 Nazi Jewish policy had reached an impasse. Military and diplomatic success had brought millions of Jews into the German sphere, while the already limited possibilities for Jewish emigration were constricted further through the outbreak of war. Germany's self-imposed "Jewish problem" mushroomed while the traditional solution collapsed. Interim solutions of massive "resettlement"—in Lublin and Madagascar—in like manner were not viable. The imminent invasion of Russia posed the same dilemma once again—further territorial conquest meant more Jews. At some point in the spring of 1941, Hitler decided to break this vicious circle.

Overwhelming documentation exists to show that Germany, under Hitler's prodding, planned and prepared for a *Vernichtungskrieg*—a war of destruction, not a conventional war—in Russia. It would be a clash of ideologies and races, not of nation-states.[28] Detailed negotiations between the army and the SS ended in an agreement with the army's promising logistical support and conceding freedom of action to small mobile SS-units—*Einsatzgruppen*—charged with "special tasks" behind German lines. All customs and international law concerning war and occupation were to be disregarded. Political commissars were to be executed. German soldiers were not to be held juridically responsible for actions against the civilian population, which was stripped of any shred of legal protection and subject to summary execution and collective reprisal. Mass starvation of millions was the anticipated result of the intended economic exploitation. Preparation for responsible care of prisoners of war was totally inadequate. Despite all that is known of German preparations for the invasion of Russia, however, specific documentation concerning the intended fate of the Russian Jews is lacking. This has led to a heated debate between Helmut Krausnick, supported by Hans-Heinrich Wilhelm on the one hand and Alfred Streim on the other, over whether the order to exterminate all Russian Jews was actually issued before the invasion or only some weeks later, in mid-summer.[29]

The controversy focused upon the proper interpretation of conflicting testimony and ambiguous documents. In their initial testimony the surviving *Einsatzkommando* leaders, with the exception of Erwin Schulz of *Einsatzkommando* 5, confirmed the Nürnberg account of Otto Ohlendorf, commander of *Einsatzgruppe* D, that an order for the destruction of the Russian Jews had been relayed to them shortly before the invasion. However, their testimony differed on whether this took place in the training camp at Pretzsch or in Berlin and whether it came from Heydrich or his chief of personnel, Bruno Streckenbach. When Streckenbach, long presumed dead, returned from Russian captivity and was promptly placed on trial, all but one of the *Einsatzkommando* leaders (Waldemar Klingelhöfer) changed their earlier testimony and subsequently denied receiving any destruction order before the invasion, from either Heydrich or Streckenbach. They now claimed that the earlier testimony had been coordinated by Ohlendorf to enable them all to plead superior orders as a defense tactic. Streim accepted the theory of an Ohlendorf conspiracy and thus the veracity of the revised testimony of these men. In was in line, he noted, with the statements of other lower-echelon *Einsatzgruppen* personnel who were first interrogated by German judicial authorities long after Nürnberg and whose testimony in this regard was more self-incriminating than perpetuating of the Ohlendorf version. Streim did admit, however, that the revised testimony was even less uniform about just how and when—the various accounts offered dates between mid-July and late August—the destruction order was finally received.[30] Krausnick in contrast did not believe the revised testimony.[31] Given the habitual mendacity of Nazi witnesses in refusing to incriminate former colleagues, a certain scepticism seems justified.

Streim attempted to bolster his case by reference to several documents. He noted that the first operation orders to the *Einsatzgruppen* referred only to the tactic of inciting pogroms by the native inhabitants against the Jews; if a destruction order had already existed, he argued, it would not have been necessary to stir up pogroms. He also noted that Heydrich's July 2 order to the Higher SS and Police Chiefs of western Russia listed only "Jews in party and state positions" among the potential enemies automatically to be shot. Streim thought that for the most part the *Einsatzgruppen* "in essence" acted within these orders, though he admitted that many Jews not within the circle of Heydrich's July 2 execution list were in fact shot before the end-of-July/end-of-August period to which he dated the general destruction order.[32] Krausnick, on the other hand, maintained that the July 2 order of Heydrich was not to be read so literally; it was, rather, a very abbreviated reference to the much more extensive verbal orders that the *Einsatzgruppen* leaders had received at their June 17 meeting in Berlin. To prove this point, Krausnick noted that not only did the *Einsatzgruppen* not stay within the narrow boundaries stipulated for shooting Jews (i.e., those in state and party positions), but also that the references in the July 2 order to *Volkstumpolitik* and the shooting of communist functionaries (in this case, only those in higher- and middle-ranking positions or classed as "radical") fell far short of the policies the *Einsatzgruppen* immediately implemented. Krausnick noted, moreover, that Operation Order Nr. 8 of July 17, 1941, which explicitly ordered the execution of all Jewish and Asiatic prisoners of war, was in fact drafted on June 28 and was being implemented before its official date of issue as well. Finally, Krausnick noted that the Tilsit *Staatspolizeistelle* was verbally informed on June 22 by the commander of *Einsatzgruppe* A, Walter Stahlecker, to shoot all Jews and suspected communists in its border region, which it proceeded to do. Krausnick did concede, however, that it was "quite possible, that the murder order was extended *explicitly* to children only toward the end of July."[33]

Streim's conclusion was that there was no single order to the *Einsatzgruppen* issued at a single time and place for the destruction of the Russian Jews; rather there were a succession of "instructions": to incite pogroms, to execute Jews in state and party positions, to carry out broader reprisals against male Jews, and finally to kill all Jews including women and children. Taken together, these composed what is retrospectively called a "Führer Order." What many of the witnesses initially referred to as the destruction orders issued at Pretzsch or Berlin were in fact only "forerunners" or "precursors" *(Vorläufer).*[34] In the limited and literal sense of day-to-day operation orders, Streim is probably right. The evidence does indicate that the *Einsatzgruppen* began hesitantly and unevenly and picked up momentum through the summer. But this does not mean that prior to the invasion there was no decision relayed through less-than-explicit exhortations to kill the Russian Jews—exhortations whose implementation was dependent upon the individual and hence nonuniform interpretation and reaction of various *Einsatzgruppen* and *Einsatzkommando* leaders.

All the testimony of these men agreed that they were subjected to a series of speeches and orientation meetings in Pretzsch and Berlin prior to the invasion, in which Heydrich and Streckenbach discussed the coming operation of the *Einsatzgruppen* at least in general terms of an ideological struggle against Bolshevism and its biological progenitor—the *Ostjuden*—as well as of the necessity for comprehensive "preventive" measures against all "potential" enemies. Clearly the *Einsatzgruppen* could kill whom they wished; but did they know from the beginning whom they should kill? The hopelessly conflicting testimony cannot clarify when and where explicit reference to killing all Jews was made. Whatever the case,

I would argue that these preinvasion sessions should not be seen as mere "precursors" of a later destruction order, as Streim sees them, but as the key point at which Heydrich conveyed to the *Einsatzgruppen* officers what was going to be expected of them. Each commander had considerable latitude to prove himself, to test the limits of local army tolerance of and cooperation with the mass murders, to incite local pogroms and enlist local collaboration, and to "ease" his men into their task. Some, like Stahlecker and Paul Blobel, proceeded more viciously and rapidly than others. A few, like Erwin Schulz, upon whose testimony Streim depends so heavily and whose experience he misleadingly generalizes, apparently did not get the point at all. Schulz noted that his unit gained a reputation for being "weak-kneed" *(schlapp)*. In early August *Einsatzgruppe* C commander Dr. Otto Rasch informed his *Kommando* leaders in Zhitomir of being reproached for treating the Jews too leniently. Higher SS and Police Chief Friedrich Jeckeln's units further behind the lines were already killing women and children, and Jeckeln had now ordered them to do likewise.[35] Even in October, Dr. Martin Sandberger of the extraordinarily murderous *Einsatzgruppe* A had killed the Jewish men but not the women and children in Estonia—a misunderstanding of his task that was subsequently remedied.[36] But Schulz and Sandberger were the exception, not the rule.

If one looks at documents written during the war rather than relying on confusing and contradictory testimony given after the war, one finds neither willingness to confess any preinvasion lack of awareness of the task the *Einsatzgruppen* were to face nor reference to any sudden postinvasion change in policy. In a summary report of events through October 15, 1941, Stahlecker wrote:

> Already in the first hours after the invasion, even if with considerable difficulty, it was possible to induce local anti-Semitic forces to pogroms against the Jews. According to orders *(befehlsgemäss)* the security police were determined to solve the Jewish question with all means and all determination. But it was not undesirable, if at least they did not appear right away in connection with the unusually hard measures that had to cause a sensation even in German circles. It had to appear to the outside, that the native population enacted the first measures on their own as a natural reaction against the decades of oppression by Jews and against the terror of the communists in the preceding period. . . . It was *expected from the start* that the Jewish problem in the Ostland would not be solved solely through pogroms. On the other hand, the security police cleansing work had *according to basic orders (gemäss grundsätzlichen Befehlen)* the goal of the most complete removal possible *(möglichst umfassende Beseitigung)* of the Jews. Extensive executions in the cities and flat lands were therefore carried out through special units. (Italics mine)

By mid-October Stahlecker's "extensive executions" had accounted for the murder of 118,430 Jews![37] In a similar vein *Sturmbannführer* Dr.

Rudolf Lange reported in January 1942: "The goal that Einsatzkommando 2 *had in mind from the beginning* was a radical solution to the Jewish problem through the execution of *all* Jews." (italics mine)[38]

In short, Krausnick and Streim focused their debate too narrowly on a specific and explicit order for the murder of all Russian Jews and thereby missed the wider question of when the *Einsatzgruppen* commanders were generally aware of the task before them. In a literal sense Streim is probably right that the lower-echelon *Einsatzgruppen* personnel received instructions to intensify the anti-Jewish measures incrementally and that the murder campaign did not take a definitive and comprehensive form until mid-summer. But in a larger sense Krausnick is right. Most—though not all—of the *Einsatzgruppen* officers were conscious of the impending genocide before the invasion. The fact that implementation would be neither instantaneous nor uniform in no way disproves this.

The question of when the *Einsatzgruppen* were *ordered* to kill the Russian Jews is, of course, different from the question of when Hitler *decided* to kill them. Precisely how and when this decision was reached remains obscure. It is not possible to determine if the initiative was Hitler's or came from someone else, such as Heydrich. Moreover, it is not possible to determine if Hitler's mind was already set by March, when he made clear to the military that the Russian war would not be a conventional war, or if the degree of military compliance tempted him subsequently to expand the circle of intended victims beyond the "Jewish-Bolshevik intelligentsia."[39] The scant documentation permits no definitive answer to these questions, merely informed speculation. Several factors suggest a March date, however. When a late March draft from the negotiations over the *Einsatzgruppen* in Russia was suddenly pressed into service to cover the jurisdiction of *Einsatzgruppen* accompanying the German invasion of Yugoslavia and Greece, "Jews and Communists" had to be specifically added to the list of categories of individuals to be "secured." Helmut Krausnick has plausibly argued that the absence of these categories for Russia would indicate that a different fate had already been decided upon for the Russian Jews analogous to the "commissar order" being prepared for Russian Communists.[40] Also, after a conference with Hitler on April 2, 1941, Rosenberg ominously noted: "What I do not want to write down today, I will nonetheless never forget."[41]

With the decision to murder the Russian Jews, Hitler broke out of the vicious circle in which each military success brought more Jews into the German sphere. This did not, however, immediately alter German Jewish policy on the rest of the continent. Emigration, expulsion, and plans for future "resettlement" still held sway. In the fall of 1940 expulsion of Jews from Baden, Pfalz, and Luxembourg took place into unoccupied France, as did deportations from Vienna to Poland in early 1941. In February 1941, Heydrich was still speaking of "sending them [the Jews] off to whatever country will be chosen later on."[42] And the Foreign Office continued to cooperate with the RSHA (Reich Security Main Office) to block Jewish emigration from other countries, so as to monopolize the limited emigration possibilities for Jews from Germany. This policy was reaffirmed as late as May 20, 1941, in a circular signed by Walter Schellenberg forbidding Jewish emigration from Belgium and France. The old policy of emigration, expulsion, and postwar "resettlement" was officially dismantled only gradually. In July 1941 the RSHA informed the Foreign Office that no further expulsions into France were intended.[43] In October Jewish emigration from Germany was forbidden. In February 1942 the Foreign Office officially canceled the Madagascar Plan. Thus the preparations for the murderous assault upon the Russian Jews did not have immediate repercussions on Nazi Jewish policy elsewhere. The emergence of the Final Solution for the European Jews was a separate process resulting from a separate though certainly not unrelated decision.

This two-decision thesis, postulating a determination for the Final Solution in Europe only after the *Einsatzgruppen* were already in action in Russia, was first articulated by Raul Hilberg in 1961. If the two-decision thesis has recently received acceptance even among some intentionalist historians, although for them simply in terms of a decision for implementation, the debate over the exact date and nature of that second decision has in contrast become increasingly heated. Thus, the remainder of this chapter will be devoted to this particular controversy.

Hilberg initially opted for a date no later than July 1941, though he now supports an August date.[44] Uwe Dietrich Adam has argued for a point between September and November. Shlomo Aronson has suggested "late fall" and Sebastian Haffner December. Martin Broszat, backed by Hans Mommsen, has challenged the whole notion of a comprehensive decision on a particular date, and has argued instead for a gradual and unconscious process of escalation. In my opinion the July date is still the most probable, provided that one understands it as merely the point at which Hitler set in motion the planning and preparation that resulted in the Final Solution.

On July 31, 1941, Heydrich received Göring's authorization to prepare a "total solution" *(Gesamtlösung)* of the Jewish question in those territories of Europe under German influence and to coordinate the participation of those organizations whose jurisdictions were touched.[45] The significance of this document is open to debate. Most historians have assumed that it refers to an extermination program. In contrast Broszat and Adam have interpreted it in terms of a "comprehensive program for the deportation of the Jews" to Russia and an attempt by Heydrich to strengthen his jurisdictional position to carry out this task, though Adam at least admits that no evidence of concrete planning in this regard has been found.[46] Indeed, the circumstances surrounding the origins of this document are uncertain. In one account Eichmann claimed that he drafted it on Heydrich's instructions, and it was then submitted for Göring's signature. In another account, however, while still assuming that the initiative came from Heydrich, Eichmann admitted: "In any case how Heydrich received this authorization I do not know."[47]

However uncertain the origins of the July authorization and however vague the phraseology about the fate intended for the Jews, this much is known. It was signed by Göring, who two weeks later expressed the opinion that "the Jews in the territories dominated by Germany had nothing more to seek." Göring did not spell out their fate further, except to say that where Jews had to be allowed to work, it could only be in closely guarded labor camps, and that he preferred that Jews be hanged rather than shot, as the latter was too honorable a death. An impending mass expulsion of Jews into Russia was neither mentioned nor implied.[48]

The authorization was received by Heydrich, who already had an authorization signed by Göring for coordinating Jewish emigration, dating from January 1939. When Jewish emigration gave way to plans for massive "resettlement," Heydrich had felt no need for a new "charter" and cited the older one when asserting jurisdiction over the emerging Madagascar Plan in 1940.[49] Moreover, Heydrich had just spent the previous months organizing the *Einsatzgruppen* for the extermination of the Russian Jews, and that murder campaign was now in full swing. The historical context would thus suggest that, if indeed Heydrich was the initiator of the July authorization, he did not need it to continue the emigration and expulsion activities over which he had long established unchallenged jurisdiction but rather because he now faced a new and awesome task that dwarfed even the systematic murder program of the *Einsatzgruppen*.

Precisely how and when Heydrich and his immediate superior, Himmler, became aware of their new task is not and probably never will be known. But given the political structure of the Third Reich, in which rival paladins vied for Hitler's favor and were successful to the degree in which they anticipated and realized his desires, and given the extermination program already underway in Russia, Himmler and Heydrich surely needed little more than a nod from Hitler to perceive that the time had come to extend the killing process to the European Jews. That such a Hitlerian incitement lay behind the July authorization cannot be definitively proven. But the testimony of Rudolf Höss and Adolf Eichmann indicates that at some point in the summer of 1941, whether in July or shortly thereafter is unclear, Himmler and Heydrich began to act on the assumption that Hitler had given them the "green light" to prepare an extermination program.

In April 1946 Rudolf Höss, the commandant of Auschwitz, stated in his initial pretrial affidavit for the International Military Tribunal that he was ordered to establish extermination facilities in June 1941.[50] He then immediately proceeded to display hopeless confusion over dates and chronology by adding that three camps in the General Government were already in operation at that time and that at Treblinka, which he had visited, eighty thousand Jews, mostly from the Warsaw ghetto, had already been killed in half a year. The General Government camps, of course, opened in the spring and summer of 1942, and deportations from Warsaw began only in July of that year. Höss had clearly confused events of the two years. Ten days later, in testimony before the International Military Tribunal, Höss dated his order to create extermination facilities at Auschwitz merely to the "summer of 1941" and claimed that Eichmann had visited about four weeks later to discuss the details.[51] In court testimony in Cracow, Poland, in November 1946, and again in his autobiography composed in February 1947, Höss's account became more detailed. "In the summer of 1941, I cannot remember the exact date," he confessed, he was summoned to Himmler who told him of the Führer order: "Every Jew that we can lay our hands on is to be destroyed now during the war, without exception."[52] Eichmann came to Auschwitz "shortly afterward" and discussed the problem of killing methods. Shooting was impossible because of the psychological burden on the executioners resulting from the large number of women and children among the victims. Gas vans already in use in the east were out of the question because of the anticipated numbers. Undecided about the particular method of gassing, Höss and Eichmann nonetheless inspected the area and chose a farmstead at Birkenau as the most suitable site. As late as November, when Höss visited Eichmann in Berlin, a suitable gas had not yet been discovered. However, Höss's assistant's use of Cyclon B on Russian prisoners of war was successful, and Höss reported its use "during Eichmann's next visit," whereupon this gas was selected for the mass extermination operation.

Some of this testimony does not withstand close scrutiny. Eichmann could not have discussed gas vans operating in the east at this time, for the prototype was not built and tested until the fall of 1941, and the first ones did not go into operation until December.[53] Furthermore, Cyclon B was first tested on Russian prisoners at Auschwitz in September, so Höss could hardly have been still in the dark about a suitable gas in November and then subsequently have agreed with Eichmann on Cyclon B during the latter's "next visit." If these aspects of the Höss account lack credibility, what remains? Comparing his testimony with that of Adolf Eichmann, at least two elements remain intact: first, that Höss learned of the decision for the extermination of the Jews sometime in the summer of 1941 but did not yet know how this was to be accomplished, and, second, that Eichmann did subsequently visit Auschwitz.

The Eichmann accounts are even more numerous than those of Höss. In the mid-1950s, while hiding in Argentina, he prepared for and gave a secret interview that surfaced in *Life Magazine* in 1960.[54] In Israel he was interrogated by the police, composed his own handwritten memoirs while awaiting trial, gave testimony in open court, and wrote various notes to his defense attorney.[55] Finally, *Ich Adolf Eichmann: Ein historischer*

Zeugenbericht, a posthumous memoir based on the material compiled for his interview in Argentina in the mid-1950s and edited by Dr. Rudolf Aschenauer, a German attorney with considerable experience in postwar trials of Nazi crimes, was published in 1980.[56]

According to the *Life Magazine* account, Eichmann learned of the destruction order in 1941 at a point when the Russian campaign was no longer going well. He added, "It was in the latter part of 1941 that I saw some of the first preparations for annihilating the Jews." On Heydrich's orders he went to Poland, where a German police captain showed him airtight "huts" to be used as gas chambers, employing carbon monoxide exhaust gas from a Russian U-boat engine. Later he witnessed an *Einsatzgruppen* execution in Minsk. By then the weather had turned "very cold," for he was wearing a long leather coat on which bits of a baby's brains were splattered and had to be cleaned off. "Later in the same winter" he was sent by Heinrich Mueller to Lodz, and witnessed the gas-van killings at nearby Chelmno. In this account Eichmann did not fit his first visit to Höss at Auschwitz into the sequence, but stated that he did visit Auschwitz "repeatedly" for he "valued Höss as an excellent comrade and a very proper fellow" whom he "liked to visit."

In his interrogation in Israel, Eichmann stated that *two or possibly three months* after the invasion of Russia, "in any case late summer," Heydrich summoned him, informed him of the Führer's order for the physical destruction of the Jews, and sent him to the SS and Police Leader in Lublin, Odilo Globocnik, to see how the latter was coming. Heydrich specifically mentioned that Globocnik was using "Russian antitank ditches," implying mass execution by the *Einsatzgruppen* method of firing squad. In Poland, however, Eichmann was taken to a camp under construction whose name he could not remember; presumably it was Belzec. Here the police captain showed him the wooden houses which would be used for gas chambers. This trip was in the fall of 1941, for Eichmann vividly remembered the bright autumn colors in the trees. He subsequently visited Minsk, where he saw the mass shootings, returned through Lemberg, where he witnessed blood spouting in little geysers from a mass grave, and finally was sent to Lodz and Chelmno, where he witnessed the gas-van killings in December 1941 or early January 1942. In addition, however, Eichmann now stated that sometime "at the beginning" he was also sent to Auschwitz, where Höss showed him the little houses in which gassing was done by pellets of Cyclon B. Unlike the first camp, where the motor to produce exhaust gas had not yet been set up and the camp was not yet in operation, in Auschwitz gassing had already been done. In his handwritten memoirs, Eichmann added two important facts concerning his visit to the first camp: one, that it was still empty and under construction when he visited, and two, that he went through Prague coming and going, where he shared all he knew with his associate, Hans Günther, on both occasions.

In court Eichmann changed only one part of the story, denying that he had been in Auschwitz before the spring of 1942. After the interrogator read Eichmann the parts of the Höss account that laid upon Eichmann the chief responsibility for selecting the gas to be used, and shifted in Eichmann's view too much of the responsibility from Pohl's Economy and Administration Head Office (WVHA) to Heydrich's Reich Security Main Office (RSHA) and from Höss to himself, Eichmann changed the date on the Auschwitz visit. As he remarked in notes to his defense attorney, "I must prove Höss the arch liar, that I had nothing at all to do with him and his gas chambers and his death camp."

Aschenauer extracts from Eichmann's notes a rather different version. The meetings with Heydrich, the latter's reference to the Führer order and Globocnik's antitank ditches, and the trip to the camp in Poland were dated to a vague "turning of the year 1941/2" (*Jahreswende* 1941/2), though neither this dating nor phrasing ever occurs in any other Eichmann account. It does, however, fit Aschenaeur's own theory, which he ceaselessly intrudes upon the reader. Aschenauer also conveniently omits any reference to the other activities of late 1941, i.e., the visits to Minsk, Lemberg, Chelmno, and possibly Auschwitz, for clearly the time necessary for all that to transpire would require an extremely elastic *Jahreswende* stretching into the fall.

If Aschenauer's version is dismissed, and I think it must be insofar as dating the events of 1941 is concerned, the major contradiction is not between Eichmann's accounts but within them. We know from other documents that Eichmann was in Prague on October 10.[57] If he visited the first camp in Poland when the fall colors were at their peak and visited Hans Günther in Prague both coming and going, this would reliably place his visit in early or mid-October. Here is where the problem arises. If his first meeting with Heydrich took place in late summer, he was not immediately sent to Poland. If he was immediately sent to Poland, as he states, this meeting with Heydrich did not take place in late summer but in late September or early October. Both are within Eichmann's time frame of two or possibly three months after the invasion of Russia. Several factors argue for the former interpretation, that considerable time passed between Eichmann's meeting with Heydrich and the first camp visit. At the meeting Heydrich spoke of plans to use antitank ditches, and Eichmann was clearly under the impression that the firing squad method of execution at the edge of mass graves was intended. This would have made Belzec a logical site; located on the Ribbentrop-Molotov line, it had earlier been the site of a Jewish labor camp for digging antitank ditches.[58] But when Eichmann arrived in Belzec, he learned for the first time of plans to use gas chambers instead of shooting. That such a fundamental change in German planning could have taken place between Eichmann's meeting with Heydrich in Berlin and an immediate trip to Poland, or that Globocnik had decided upon gas chambers without Heydrich's knowledge, seems unlikely. That Eichmann learned from Heydrich of Hitler's order for the destruction of the Jews in late August, more than a month before the October trip, is also suggested by Eichmann's letter of August 28, 1941, which adds to the old formulation about the "imminent Final Solution" the ominous phrase "now in preparation." (The entire formulation now read *"im Hinblick auf die kommende und in Vorbereitung befindliche Endlösung."*)[59] That this plan "now in preparation" did not involve mass "resettlement" in Russia as hypothesized by Adam and Broszat is indicated by Eichmann's reply two weeks later to a Foreign Office inquiry over the possibility of deporting Serbian Jews to the east. The Foreign Office notation of Eichmann's telephone response reads: "According to the information of *Sturmbannführer* Eichmann . . . residence in Russia and GG [General Government] impossible. Not even the Jews from Germany can be lodged there. Eichmann proposes shooting." *(Nach Auskunft Sturmbannführer Eichmann RSHA IV D VI* [sic], *Aufenhalt in Russland und GG unmöglich. Nicht einmal die Juden aus Deutschland können dort untergebracht werden. Eichmann schlägt Erschiessen vor.)*[60] In conclusion, the Eichmann testimony cannot exactly date the point at which Eichmann was fully conscious of the intention to murder the European Jews, but his awareness probably dates from late August and cannot be postponed beyond the end of September/beginning of October. This, I would argue, also lends plausibility to Höss's account that he too learned of the plans sometime in the summer of 1941.

In September the German Jews were marked. In October, further emigration was forbidden; the first deportations of German Jews to Lodz occurred; and Slovakia, Croatia, and Rumania were asked to permit the inclusion of Jews of their citizenship residing in Germany in these deportations just getting underway. In November the Eleventh Decree to the Reich Citizenship Law provided for the loss of citizenship and forfeit of property of Jews residing outside German borders. Such preparatory measures, admittedly, would have been necessary whether the German Jews were fated at this time merely for deportation or for extermination. However, a few surviving documents from October 1941 support the testimony of Eichmann and Höss that planning activities now focused on the ultimate goal of extermination, not just deportation. A number of Spanish Jews had been arrested and interned in France, which led the Spanish to suggest the possibility of evacuating all Spanish Jews in France (some two thousand) to Spanish Morocco. On October 13, Foreign Office Undersecretary Martin Luther urged negotiations in that direction—a position fully in line with the prevailing policy of achieving a *judenrein* Europe through the expulsion of the Jews. Four days later, however, Heydrich's RSHA informed Luther by telephone of its opposition to the Spanish proposal, as the Spanish government had neither the will nor the experience effectively to guard the Jews in Morocco. "In addition these Jews would also be too much out of the direct reach of the *measures for a basic solution to the Jewish question to be enacted after the war."* *(Darüber hinaus wären diese Juden aber auch bei den nach Kreigsende zu ergreifenden Mass-nahmen zur gründsätzlichen Lösung der Judenfrage dem unmittelbaren Zugriff allzusehr entzogen.)*[61] (Italics mine) The rejection of deportation to Morocco combined with the mention of a basic solution to be enacted after the war, which prior removal of the Jews would thwart, indicated that a fundamental shift in Nazi Jewish policy had occurred. Within the SS a *judenfrei* Europe was no longer being pursued through expulsion.

Also in October 1941 Eichmann's associate, Friedrich Suhr, accompanied the Foreign Office Jewish expert, Franz Rademacher, to Belgrade to deal with the Jewish question in Serbia. After the fate of the adult male Jews was settled (they were shot by army firing squad in reprisal for casualties suffered from partisan attacks), Rademacher reported on the women, children, and elderly: "Then as soon as the technical possibility exists within the framework of a total solution of the Jewish question, the Jews will be deported by waterway to the reception camp in the east." *(Sobald dann im Rahmen der Gesamtlösung der Judenfrage die tech-nische Möglichkeit besteht, werden die Juden auf dem Wasserwege in die Auffanglager im Osten abgeschoben.)*[62] Just after learning of plans for a reception camp in the east at a conference attended by one of Eichmann's closest associates, Rademacher received a letter from Paul Wurm, foreign editor of *Der Stürmer:*

> Dear Party Comrade Rademacher!
> On my return trip from Berlin I met an old party comrade who works in the east on the settlement of the Jewish question. In the near future many of the Jewish vermin will be exterminated through special measures. *(Auf meiner Rückreise aus Berlin traf ich einen alten Parteigenossen, der im Osten an der Regelung der Judenfrage arbeitet. In nächster Zeit wird von dem jüdischen Ungeziefer durch besondere Massnahmen manches vernich-tet werden.)*[63]

Together these documents would indicate that the Jewish experts coming to and from Berlin in the month of October were aware of plans for a "reception camp" in the east to receive Jews incapable of heavy labor, and of "special measures" for extermination. The exact location of the planned reception camp was not clear, though the reference to transport by waterway would suggest that a Danube–Black Sea route to Russia was being considered.

Discussion of both gassing and the creation of new camps for Jews in Russia was recorded on yet another occasion in October by *Ostminis-terium* Jewish expert Alfred Wetzel, who met with Eichmann and euthanasia supervisor Viktor Brack.[64] Brack advised the construction of gassing apparatus, presumably gas vans, on the spot because they were not in sufficient supply in the Reich.[65] Brack offered to send his chemist Dr. Kallmeyer to help out. Eichmann confirmed that Jewish camps were about to be set up in Riga and Minsk to receive German Jews. Those capable of labor would be sent "to the east" later, but he saw no reason "why those Jews who are not fit for work should not be removed by the Brack method" in the meantime.

Riga and Minsk were also mentioned as destinations for deported Jews at an October 10 conference in Prague chaired by Heydrich. At this same conference Heydrich noted that "Nebe and Rasch could take in Jews in the camps for communist prisoners in the theater of operations." Perhaps Heydrich meant Stahlecker and Nebe, the respective *Einsatzgruppen* commanders in Riga and Minsk. In any case the fact that deported Jews were to be turned over to the *Einsatzgruppen* commanders, who were supervising the killing of Jews and communists, indicates that even in early October Heydrich was not in doubt about the specific fate of these deportees.[66]

These October documents do not yet portray the Final Solution in its definitive form, but they do suggest that frenetic planning was underway and that key ingredients of the Final Solution—special reception camps for the deported Jews and gassing—were being discussed among the Jewish experts not only in the SS but also in the Führer's Chancellory, Foreign Office, and *Ostministerium*. These documents thus enhance the credibility of Eichmann and Höss and the contention that a gradually widening circle of Nazi Jewish experts was becoming conscious that the ultimate goal was no longer "resettlement" but rather extermination.

In addition to documentary evidence and the testimony of Höss and Eichmann, circumstantial evidence should be considered as well. Is it plausible that in October the Nazis were setting in motion a vast program of deportation, while still unaware of its implications and undecided about the ultimate fate of the deportees? The SS had already been forced to call off deportations to the Lublin Reservation in the spring of 1940 because limited but indiscriminate deportation of Jews without careful preparation had proved chaotic and unfeasible. There was no desire for a repetition of that fiasco, yet the attempt to resettle Europe's entire Jewish population in Russia would have had far graver consequences. German planners acknowledged openly and frequently that exploitation of Russian food supplies was going to entail the mass starvation of native inhabitants. A meeting of state secretaries on May 2, 1941, noted that "umpteen million people will doubtless starve to death, when we extract what is necessary for us from the country."[67] The *Wirtschaftsstab Ost* report of May 23, 1941, stated that the population of the northern forest region

> especially the urban population, will inevitably face a great famine. . . .
> Many tens of millions of people will be superfluous in this area and will die or have to emigrate to Siberia. Attempts to rescue the population there from famine by drawing upon surpluses from the black earth region can only be at the expense of provisioning Europe. They endanger Germany's capacity to hold out in the war, they endanger Germany's resistance to blockade. Absolute clarity must prevail in this regard.[68]

The report also noted that the problem of emigration to Siberia would be "extremely difficult" because "rail transportation was out of the question." And in August Göring "reckoned with great loss of life on nutritional grounds."[69] Was anyone seriously considering a massive influx of additional people into Russia under these circumstances without being clear about the consequences?

When the SS Jewish experts began seriously to consider the Madagascar resettlement in the summer of 1940, they produced within two months a neatly printed brochure, complete with table of contents and maps, outlining the future governance and economy of the "super-ghetto."[70] However fantastic the Madagascar Plan may have been, the planners were men who clearly thought beyond the initial stage of deportation. By 1941 they could have had few illusions about the practical difficulties of solving the Jewish question. It is inconceivable that they spent the autumn of 1941 wrestling with the obstacles to deportation while undecided about the most important problem of all—the disposition of the deportees.

Given the already apparent inadequacies of the *Einsatzgruppen* operations—their inefficiency, the lack of secrecy, and the psychological burden on the executioners—and their even greater unsuitability for use outside Russia, the most important problem Himmler and Heydrich faced was how and where to kill the Jews. Ultimately the Nazi planners solved this problem by merging three already existing programs with which they had prior experience: the concentration camp system, euthanasia gassing, and Eichmann's specialty of forced emigration and population resettlement. Auschwitz, because of its rail connections, was chosen as one site for a killing center. The possibility of other sites in Russia may have been weighed until the military and transportation situation made this unfeasible. The exact type of gas to be used remained undetermined; in the end the Polish camps manned by euthanasia personnel retained carbon monoxide while Auschwitz and Maidanek adopted Cyclon B.

When was this solution—deportation to camps equipped with gassing facilities—finally approved? The answer lies in another question: When did the construction of the first death camps and the initial shifting of euthanasia personnel begin? The course of events at Auschwitz is not helpful in validating the date, for Auschwitz was already a labor camp at which many Russian prisoners of war were being systematically killed. The gassing of some of these Russian prisoners in September 1941 with Cyclon B in Bunker 11 at the *Stammlager* was followed by at least several gassings of small contingents of local Jews in the "old crematory." However, the gassing of large transports of Jews in the converted farm house at Birkenau did not begin until late January 1942.[71] This sequence provides no clear indication as to when Höss was first aware of this new killing task. Belzec and Chelmno, however, provide a better check, for neither was then in existence as an operating labor camp and both were constructed solely to kill Jews. The date when construction on these camps began can thus provide a crucial check as to when a significant number of Germans knew what they were about in preparing for the Final Solution. Most of the German defendants in the Belzec and Chelmno trials were not at those camps at the beginning and could provide no relevant testimony. However, the testimony of two German defendants in this regard, corroborated by the testimony of local inhabitants in those areas taken by the Poles immediately after the war, clearly points once again to October 1941.

Let us examine the Chelmno evidence first. Since early 1940 a *Sonderkommando* under Herbert Lange, headquartered in Posen, had been carrying out euthanasia operations in East Prussia and the incorporated territories. According to Lange's chauffeur, he drove the *Sonderkommando* chief around the Warthegau in the fall of 1941 searching for a suitable location for a death camp. He then drove Lange to Berlin and back, arriving in Chelmno in late October or early November. Thereafter a team of SS men was assembled from Posen and Lodz, followed by a guard detachment of Order Police. A work force of Polish prisoners from Lodz together with local inhabitants was put to work renovating and fencing the old villa or *Schloss,* where the Jews would be undressed and loaded into the waiting gas vans. After preparations were complete, the gassing began on December 8.[72]

Polish postwar interrogations of the *Volksdeutsche* (ethnic German) inhabitants of the village provide the same sequence. According to the *Amtskommissar* of Chelmno, he was away from town toward the end of 1941 when some SS men arrived and investigated the *Schloss* and other buildings. Some days later, after his return, Lange appeared and confiscated various buildings. Lange returned still later with a team of SS-men, followed by police. Some weeks after the arrival of the SS-unit, work on the *Schloss* was complete and the first truckloads of Jews arrived.[73] Such a sequence of events would necessitate Lange's having received his initial instructions to establish a death camp at Chelmno no later than mid- or late October but more likely toward the beginning of the month.

The sequence of events at Belzec leads to much the same conclusion. Again we have the testimony of only one German defendant, Josef Oberhauser, initially an employee of the euthanasia program and subsequently adjutant to Christian Wirth, the inspector of the Polish death camps of Operation Reinhard. Oberhauser was assigned to Globocnik in Lublin in October and arrived there in November 1941. His first job consisted of bringing to Belzec building materials as well as Ukrainian guardsmen from their training camp at Trawniki. He was in no doubt as to what was intended in Belzec, as the construction supervisor showed him the plans for the gas chamber. By Christmas the initial construction was finished, and Oberhauser became Wirth's liaison to Globocnik. After the first gassing test killed fifty Jewish workers, Wirth went to Berlin for six weeks. Upon his return in March, the first transports began to arrive.[74]

According to local inhabitants, three SS men came to Belzec in October 1941 and demanded a draft of twenty Polish workers. Work began on November 1 under the direction of a young ethnic German *Baumeister* from Kattowitz, who supervised the construction according to a set of plans. After putting up two barracks and the future gas chamber near the railway siding, the Polish workers were dismissed on December 23. By then black-uniformed former Russian prisoners of war had arrived to carry on the work and guard seventy Jewish laborers. After more barracks, guard towers, and fencing were completed, the Jewish workers were killed in the first test of the gassing facilities in February 1942. Full-time operations then began in March.[75] Thus not only is the Oberhauser testimony confirmed, but an Eichmann visit to an empty camp at Belzec in October 1941 and his reception by a lone police captain fits this sequence of events precisely. The few wooden buildings he saw must have dated from the former Jewish labor camp at Belzec.

While many euthanasia personnel were sent from Germany to Russia in the winter of 1941–1942 and were not reassigned to the death camps until the spring of 1942, some key personnel were already involved earlier. Not only had Wirth and Oberhauser been sent from Berlin in the fall of 1941, but Brack also dispatched to Lublin his chemist, Dr. Helmut Kallmeyer, the man he had unsuccessfully tried to send to Riga in late October. Kallmeyer admitted being sent to Lublin after Christmas, but said no one had had any use for him and he had been quickly sent back.[76] SS-*Untersturmführer* Dr. August Becker, on loan from the SS to the euthanasia program since January 1940 for the purpose of delivering bottled carbon monoxide to the euthanasia institutes, testified frankly (when terminally ill and no longer facing trial): "Himmler wanted to use the people released from euthanasia who were experts in gassing, such as myself, in the great gassing program getting underway in the east." Before being assigned in December 1941 to supervise gas vans operating with the *Einsatzgruppen* in Russia, Becker had already heard talk in Berlin that other members of the euthanasia program were being sent to Lublin to start "something similar," only this time according to rumor it would be for the Jews.[77]

If the October documents cited above indicate that middle echelon officials of the Führer's Chancellory, Foreign Office, and *Ostministerium* were then discussing special reception camps and gassing in relation to the Jews, the Chelmno and Belzec testimony indicates that, within the SS, preparation for constructing the death camps was in fact already getting underway in that month. Such evidence makes *very compelling* the conclusion that *by October* Hitler had approved the mass-murder plan. It must be kept in mind, however, that the death-camp solution was not self-evident; it had to be invented. Precisely how long the whole process of initiation, invention, and approval took, we do not know. In the accounts of Eichmann and Höss, they learned from Heydrich and Himmler respectively by late summer of 1941 of Hitler's order to destroy the Jews but not yet how that was to be accomplished. If the death-camp solution had been approved and was being implemented in October, it is at least *very probable* that the problem was first posed by Himmler and Heydrich to others in August, and that they themselves were first incited to the task by Hitler in late July.

Furthermore, the evidence concerning the founding of the death camps at Chelmno and Belzec does not support the hypothesis of the primacy of local initiative but rather indicates considerable interaction with central authorities in Berlin. Both camps involved the reassignment of personnel formerly involved in the euthanasia program, which was coordinated in the Führer's Chancellory. Both commandants, Lange and Wirth, made trips back to Berlin before their camps began operating. Both camps received visits from Eichmann on inspection tour from Berlin. Both utilized killing technology developed in Germany—in Belzec the stationary gas chamber on the euthanasia institute model, and in Chelmno the gas van, which was developed, tested, produced, and dispatched with drivers by the RSHA.[78]

These conclusions are not compatible with the theories of Adam and Haffner, who date the decision for the Final Solution to the fall or winter of 1941, nor with Broszat's thesis of the primacy of local initiative in setting the process in motion. Central to all these theories is the conviction that the failure of the Russian campaign was crucial in launching the Final Solution: either in forcing Hitler to choose different priorities, as in Haffner's case, or in forcing the Germans to find a solution to the Jewish question other than "resettlement" in Russia, as with Adam and Broszat. If the death camps were already approved and the initial steps were being taken in October, the process involved in launching the Final Solution had to have begun much earlier, at a point when victory in Russia was still expected by the end of the year. Aronson's dating of "late fall," sometime after the implications of American Lend-Lease to Russia had altered Hitler's outlook, likewise is too late to account for this course of events unless the time between the change he postulates in Hitler's thinking and the commencement of death-camp construction were almost instantaneous. It would appear that the euphoria of victory in the summer of 1941 and the intoxicating vision of all Europe at their feet, not the dashed expectations and frustrations of the last months of the year, induced the Nazis to set the fateful process in motion.

Certainly the subsequent behavior of various Nazi leaders is compatible with this thesis of October as the approval date for the Final Solution. On October 30, Heydrich sent to the Foreign Office the first five "Activity and Situation Reports on the *Einsatzgruppen* of the Sipo-SD in Russia," which detailed the massacres that had taken place the previous summer. As the Foreign Office copy was often only one of as many as one hundred copies, such information was being widely circulated.[79] Perhaps Heydrich's timing was fortuitous. Or perhaps he was attuning recipients to the "new realities," psychologically preparing them for participation in the Final Solution. On November 11, Himmler told Kersten that "the destruction of the Jews is being planned. . . . Now the destruction of the Jews is imminent."[80] On November 18 Rosenberg gave a "confidential" background report to the German press and asserted that the Jewish question "can only be solved in a biological extermination *(Ausmerzung)* of all Jews in Europe."[81] On November 25 in Kovno and November 30 in Riga, deported German Jews were massacred for the first time. On November 29, Heydrich issued his invitations to the Wannsee Conference, originally scheduled for December 9 but postponed until January 20, 1942. And on December 14, Rosenberg recorded a conversation with Hitler: "I took the viewpoint not to speak of the extermination *(Ausrottung)* of the Jews. The Führer approved this attitude."[82]

For many who had been waiting anxiously for direction from Berlin on the Jewish question, December was a month of resolution. An inquiry from the *Reichskommissariat* Ostland as to whether all Jews should be liquidated regardless of age, sex, and economic interest was answered from Berlin on December 18: "In the meantime clarity on the Jewish question has been achieved through oral discussion: economic interests are to be disregarded on principle in the settlement of this problem."[83] On December 16 Hans Frank, who had sent his State Secretary Josef Bühler to Berlin to find out what was behind the Wannsee invitation, reported to his followers in the General Government that the Polish Jews could not be deported; thus they would have to be liquidated. He did not know exactly how, but measures should be taken "in connection with the great measures to be discussed in the Reich" to accomplish this task. If unsure of the method, Frank had no doubt of the goal: *"Wir müssen die Juden vernichten."* [We must destroy the Jews.][84]

Heydrich's Wannsee Conference invitation of November 29, 1941, contained a copy of Göring's July 31 authorization.[85] At the conference Heydrich invoked not only it but also "previous approval through the Führer."[86] All Jews, Heydrich announced, would be deported to the east for labor. Most would disappear through "natural diminution." The survivors, the hardiest, would be "treated accordingly," for no Jews were to survive "as a germ cell of a new Jewish reconstruction." That the participants were clear that the real goal of the vast deportation program was extermination, not labor, can be seen from the request of State Secretary Bühler of the General Government that the Final Solution begin in Poland because most of the Jews there were already incapable of work.

If the goal and scope of German Jewish policy was no longer in doubt, some aspects of the Final Solution were still unsettled. "Practical experience" of significance to the Final Solution was being gathered, and "possible solutions" were discussed, which Eichmann confirmed to have been a discussion of "killing possibilities."[87] Though the Chelmno gas vans were already operating, and the makeshift facilities at Auschwitz were just being put into operation, apparently it was not until mid-March, with the opening of Belzec, that the gas chamber passed the final test. The proportion of those to be worked to death and those killed immediately was left open and remained a source of contention throughout. The issues of *Mischlinge* and German Jews in mixed marriage, which took up much of the conference, would never be definitively resolved. Nevertheless, despite these unanswered questions, the extermination of the European Jews as the ultimate goal of German Jewish policy had been revealed to a significantly wider circle in order to assure needed cooperation.

One must not, however, overemphasize the degree of coherency and clarity in Nazi Jewish policy in this crucial period from the summer of 1941 to the spring of 1942. In addition to the issues still unresolved at the time of the Wannsee Conference, two further factors confused the situation: (1) Hitler's decision to deport German Jews in the fall of 1941 superimposed upon the planners an additional task before the plan for a European-wide solution to the Jewish question and the means of implementing that plan were ready. (2) The method of transmitting information about policy changes within the Third Reich was very unsystematic, and the process by which people and institutions were initiated into the new policy was gradual and irregular. Hence considerable uncertainty, confusion, and ignorance surrounded German Jewish policy in the fall of 1941. This has led some historians to argue that the ultimate aim of German Jewish policy was still very much undecided.

Consider, first, the fall deportations from Germany. Göring's July authorization referred to a plan for the entire German sphere of influence in Europe and came at a time when rapid German victory over Russia was still assumed. In August, before such a plan could be devised and while expectations of imminent victory were still alive, Hitler resisted pressure from Heydrich and Goebbels and rejected deportations from Germany "during the war."[88] As late as September 13, Eichmann likewise told the Foreign Office that no deportation of Serbian Jews to the General Government or Russia was possible, for not even German Jews could be lodged there.[89] By then, however, prospects of total German victory that fall were less certain, and Hitler appears to have made a snap decision, reversing himself. On September 14, Rosenberg urged Hitler to approve the immediate deportation of German Jews in retaliation for the Russian deportation of Volga Germans to Siberia. Four days later Himmler informed Greiser, *Gauleiter* of the Wartheland, of interim deportations to Lodz, because the Führer wished to make the Old Reich and Protectorate *judenfrei* as soon as possible, hopefully by the end of the year.[90] Shortly thereafter Heydrich similarly announced in Prague the Führer's wish that insofar as possible the German Jews were to be deported to Lodz, Riga, and Minsk by the end of the year.[91]

Thus, in addition to their efforts to devise a Final Solution to the Jewish question in all Europe, the planners suddenly had to improvise immediate deportations as an interim solution for the Reich. The attempt to carry out these deportations before the death camps now being conceived were built caused difficulties and confusion. German authorities in the reception areas resisted the unwelcome influx, despite assurances that it was all temporary and the Jews would be sent "to the east" in the spring,[92] because these intended way stations did not have the capacity to take on such numbers even for a half year. But however confusing and unsuccessful these improvised deportations may have been, their ultimate failure was not the cause of the Final Solution, as has been suggested by Adam and Broszat. The evidence shows that the Germans were working on the extermination program even while these deportations were just beginning.

Consider, next, the issue of information-flow within the Third Reich. Broszat has argued that the absence of any reference to a specific Hitler order for the Final Solution in the postwar testimony or surviving diaries of leading Nazis casts doubt upon the existence of a definitive Hitler decision for the Final Solution. The unsystematic and irregular flow of information was, however, a pervasive feature of the political system of the Third Reich. Ignorance about current Jewish policy among some high-ranking Nazis in no way precludes a clear understanding in the minds of others of Hitler's desires in this regard. The examples of Joseph Goebbels and Joachim von Ribbentrop, the ministers of Propaganda and Foreign Affairs, are most illustrative in this regard. Goebbels had long attempted to play a role in Jewish affairs. His instigation of the *Kristallnacht* pogrom had led, however, to the centralization of Jewish policy under the rival triumvirate of Göring, Himmler, and Heydrich. In the summer of 1941 Goebbels again sought a role. On August 15 he addressed a meeting at the Propaganda Ministry on the question of marking. After blaming the Jews for everything from the lack of housing to the strawberry shortage in Berlin, he suggested a series of measures: sending the nonworking Jews to Russia, cutting their rations, or, best of all, killing them! *(am besten wäre es, diese überhaupt totzuschlagen.)* Basic to any measures, however, was the marking of the Jews, Goebbels argued, and by August 20, he had secured Hitler's agreement to this preparatory measure. Goebbels's attempted power-grab was only partially successful, for despite his initiative in this matter, the SS retained jurisdiction over the marking decree that ensued.[93]

While Goebbels may have constantly agitated for a more radical Jewish policy, he was seldom the designer or executor of these policies. Heydrich jealously guarded his prerogatives, and no representative from the Ministry of Propaganda was invited to the Wannsee Conference. Only six weeks later, presumably in connection with the *Mischlinge* conference of March 6 (which one of Goebbels's men did attend), did the Propaganda Ministry receive a report, and an expurgated one at that. On March 7, 1942, Goebbels noted in his diary:

> I read a detailed report from the SD and police regarding the final solution of the Jewish question. Any final solution involves a tremendous number of new viewpoints. The Jewish question must be solved within a pan-European frame. There are 11,000,000 Jews still in Europe. They will have to be concentrated later, to begin with, in the East; possibly an island, such as Madagascar, can be assigned to them after the war.[94]

In contrast, the Foreign Office received its copy of the unexpurgated Wannsee Conference protocol (one of thirty) on January 26, and even the low-echelon officials of the Colonial desk were informed by February 10 that the Madagascar Plan was defunct.[95] Clearly much about Nazi Jewish policy was being kept from Goebbels, and his first awareness of the Final Solution was recorded only on March 27, 1942, several weeks after Belzec began operating.[96]

If the intense competition of the Nazi political system caused a very uneven flow of information through the government, as rivals deliberately withheld information from one another, Hitler's informal and irregular manner of governing contributed to the same result. There was no written order for the Final Solution nor any explicit reference to a verbal order other than the assertions of Himmler and Heydrich that they were acting with the Führer's approval.[97] Participation in the Final Solution did not result so much from explicit orders systematically disseminated as through self-recruitment by the zealous and ambitious servants of the Third Reich in response to the impulses and hints they perceived emanating from the centers of power. If a nod from Hitler could set Himmler and Heydrich in motion, others eagerly looked for similar signs. A classic example of self-recruitment by the clever and ambitious coexisting with enduring ignorance on the part of the obtuse is provided by Undersecretary Martin Luther and his boss, Foreign Minister Ribbentrop. Luther was a man with a sensitive hand on the political pulse of the Third Reich. Keenly aware of the signs of change in Nazi Jewish policy in the fall of 1941, Luther quickly closed ranks with his old antagonist, Heydrich, to secure a role for the Foreign Office and prevent a further diminution of its dwindling influence. Invited to the Wannsee Conference, Luther did not inform Ribbentrop of this until the following summer. Even then the foreign minister, though certainly aware of large numbers of Jews being killed (he had received summaries of the *Einsatzgruppen* reports from Luther), seemed unable to perceive the scope of the Final Solution and the importance Hitler attached to it. Piqued by SS encroachments on his jurisdiction, Ribbentrop temporarily ordered his Foreign Office to cease pressing Germany's allies on the deportation question. Only Hitler's vehemence on the Jewish question during back-to-back visits in September 1942 by the Croatian head of state, Ante Pavelič, and the Rumanian deputy prime minister, Mihai Antonescu, sent the obsequious Ribbentrop scurrying to the telephone to cancel this order. However, it was not until the Luther Putsch in February 1943 misfired, when Himmler backed Ribbentrop instead of his undersecretary, that Ribbentrop finally perceived the political expediency of engaging in personal diplomacy on behalf of the Final Solution.[98]

Thus the circle of initiates widened in a very unsystematic manner. The cleverest perceived the signs of change and recruited themselves to the new policy. Others were brought in as their services were needed, such as at the Wannsee Conference. Some appear to have been deliberately excluded. And some were simply too stupid or blind to see what was going on. The bizarre result was that lower-ranking officials in certain areas of the government knew more than some top-ranking Nazis elsewhere. Thus different Nazis, loyal to Hitler, anti-Semitic to the core, could pursue different policies and make contradictory statements regarding the Jews with the full conviction that they acted with the Führer's blessing. This was not a state of affairs Hitler sought to correct. Indeed, given his cynical tongue-in-cheek comments during this period, he set the tone and deliberately encouraged a policy of maximum ambiguity.[99] Such confusion has obscured the origins of the Final Solution but ultimately cannot disguise the fact that Hitler, Göring, Himmler, and Heydrich knew what they were trying to do since the summer of 1941. The circle of initiates widened steadily if irregularly thereafter.

In conclusion, there was no Hitler order from which the Final Solution sprang full grown like Athena from the head of Zeus. But sometime in the summer of 1941, probably before Göring's July 31 authorization, Hitler gave Himmler and Heydrich the signal to draw up a destruction plan, the completion of which inevitably involved the exploration of various alternatives, false starts, and much delay. Considerable "lead time" was needed, for the Nazis were venturing into uncharted territory and attempting the unprecedented; they had no maps to follow—hence, a seeming ambivalence surrounding German Jewish policy in the late summer and autumn of 1941, which was aggravated by two factors. The first was the decision in mid-September to deport German Jews before the new killing facilities had been devised. The second was the Byzantine style of government in which initiative from above was informal, information was shared irregularly, and uncertainty was often deliberately cultivated. By October, a not unreasonable two or three months after Hitler had given the green light to proceed, the pieces were falling together. Many outside the SS were now involved, and there had emerged the rough outline of a plan involving mass deportation to killing centers that used poison gas. The first concrete steps for implementing this plan—beginning construction of the earliest death camps at Belzec and Chelmno and the first transfer of euthanasia personnel, both inconceivable without Hitler's approval—were taken by the end of the month. The decision for the Final Solution had been confirmed.

2
Wehrmacht Reprisal Policy
and the Murder of the Male Jews
in Serbia

In the fall of 1941, Wehrmacht firing squads, with help from the local Security and Order Police, shot the adult male Jews in Serbia. While very valuable and important scholarship has emerged in recent years on Wehrmacht participation in the *Vernichtungskrieg* in Russia,[1] the Wehrmacht role in the murder of the Serbian Jews has not been sufficiently clarified in either scholarship or judicial proceedings.[2] It is my contention that although these shootings were carried out within the framework of a reprisal policy developed in response to the partisan uprising and were not part of the European-wide genocide program, which in any case was still in the planning stages, the Wehrmacht in fact dealt with Jewish hostages differently than with Serbs solely because they were Jews. The resulting massacre of these Jews was primarily the responsibility of the military commanders in Serbia, not the local SS, Wilhelm Keitel and the OKW (High Command of the Armed Forces), or central authorities in Berlin.

The German occupation structure in Serbia was exceedingly complex. A Luftwaffe general—first Ludwig von Schröder, then Heinrich Danckelmann—served as *Militärbefehlshaber in Serbien,* responsible to the Military Commander Southeast in Greece, Field Marshal Wilhelm List. The *Militärbefehlshaber* had two staffs. The first was the administrative staff or *Verwaltungsstab* under State Councillor and SS-*Gruppenführer* Harald Turner and his deputy, SS-*Sturmbannführer* Georg Kiessel, which supervised the activities of the Serbian provisional government, the four *Feldkommandanturen* or districts into which Serbia had been divided, the Sipo-SD *Einsatzgruppe* of SS-*Standartenführer* Wilhelm Fuchs, and the 64th Reserve Police Battalion of Order Police. The second was the command staff of Lieutenant Colonel Gravenhorst, through which the *Militär-befehlshaber* exercised a direct control over the regional defense battalions and a more distant control over General Paul Bader's 65th Corps. In addition to the military and SS presence in Serbia, Göring's Four Year Plan was represented through a plenipotentiary for the economy, Hans Neuhausen, and the Foreign Office was represented by yet another plenipotentiary, Ambassador Felix Benzler. This plethora of German occupation authorities,[3] along with List in Greece and Keitel of the OKW, was responsible for shaping the German response to the partisan war in Serbia.

The communist uprising that took place in German-occupied Serbia following the invasion of Russia on June 22, 1941, did not take the Germans by surprise, but it was expected in terms of small-group banditry that could be dealt with by the police, not as a large-scale military threat necessitating army involvement. There was in fact a conscious aim to avoid the use of German troops, for the three divisions in Serbia were understrength (two instead of three regiments), overaged, poorly equipped, widely dispersed, immobile, and still in training.[4] Among the initial police measures taken to combat the communist resistance activity were reprisal executions of arrested Communist suspects. In addition, Jews were prominent among the earliest reprisal victims. Immediately following the Yugoslav defeat, the German occupation regime had imposed severe restrictions upon the Serbian Jews, including registration, exclusion from many occupations and social activities, expropriation of property, marking, and forced labor. After the invasion of Russia the Jewish community had to provide 40 hostages weekly, and Jews were explicitly included among the 111 people executed in German reprisals by July 22, though the exact number was not specified in the German statistics.[5]

In late July Schröder disseminated guidelines for "deterrent" and "expiatory" measures which had been prepared by the administrative staff.[6] The guidelines imposed many restrictions: special care was to be taken to investigate the facts of any incident, for "measures unjustly enacted damage German prestige" *(Massnahmen, die zu Unrecht getroffen sind, schaden dem deutschen Ansehen);* reprisal shooting was to occur only for actions committed after the hostages had been arrested and sufficient warning had been given; a close connection between the hostages and the perpetrators had to exist; and the decision of the military commander was needed in every case. However, the guidelines also permitted measures against the population of a location if they made themselves "coresponsible" *(mitverantwortlich)* by facilitating sabotage committed by others, by passively resisting German investigation, or by offering fertile soil to anti-German activity. Thus in addition to arrested Communists and the Jewish hostage pool from which reprisal victims had been selected so far, Serbians on the spot deemed coresponsible were now vulnerable. The first use of this new reprisal policy occurred on July 27, when Serbian police were forced at gunpoint to shoot eighty-one harvest workers rounded up in the fields near the site of an ambushed German car.[7]

As German police measures proved inadequate in stemming the growth of the partisan movement, the occupation authorities sought a more effective counterinsurgency policy. Field Marshal List visited Serbia on July 21 and 22 and ordered the troops of Bader's 65th Corps to take a more active combat role.[8] The OKW exhorted more intensive repression; the military commander was expected to "burn out the troublemakers through the most brutal actions and sharpest reprisals" *(durch brutales Einschreiten und schaerfste Repressalien die Unruheherde ausbrennt)* and to hang, not shoot, saboteurs.[9] In contrast to greater military involvement or more draconic reprisals, a number of local German officials of the army, military administration, police, and Foreign Office preferred expanded police measures, with particular emphasis on a strengthened and better-armed Serbian police.[10] German policy in Serbia would in practice embrace all these options but vacillate in emphasis as none initially brought success.

On July 27 Schröder died of injuries suffered in a plane crash and was replaced by another Luftwaffe commander, General Danckelmann. On August 2, Danckelmann informed List that he intended to proceed in the future primarily with police actions and use troops only in exceptional cases. The following day he foolishly announced that he was "master of the situation" and needed no reinforcements.[11] He was quickly stripped of his illusions, but his subsequent requests for more police and a full division were both turned down.[12] The lack of reinforcements for a military solution was compounded by the imminent collapse of the Serbian police upon whom so many of the Germans in Serbia had hoped to shift the main burden of antipartisan operations. Ill-equipped and demoralized, the Serbian police could no longer be relied upon to carry the burden of pacification.[13]

If the forces of the German military and Serbian police seemed increasingly inadequate, the reprisal policy begun on local initiative and then emphatically endorsed by the OKW was proving not only inadequate but counterproductive. Numerous German documents make clear that Schröder's initial injunction to avoid injustices was a dead letter and that German reprisal policy was not contributing to pacification. Instead it was driving peaceful, politically indifferent, and loyal portions of the Serbian population into bitterness and despair and ultimately into the ranks of the insurgents.[14] Despite numerous warnings to this effect, draconic reprisal measures remained an essential part of German strategy. When Danckelmann ordered the formation of mobile pursuit companies in mid-August, List's chief of staff, Hermann Foertsch, emphasized the need not only for mobility but also for such measures as hostage shootings, hangings, and threats to local authorities, family members, and landlords of suspected insurgents.[15] This was not empty rhetoric. For an ambush of a German police car in Skela two days later, fifty Communists were hanged in Belgrade, fifteen villagers were shot for not reporting the presence of the partisans, and the entire village of 350 houses was burned to the ground. When Kiessel objected that no investigation had been made to ascertain the facts, Gravenhorst referred to a specific authorization from Foertsch to proceed with such severe measures.[16]

The pace of arbitrary reprisals did not slacken, nor did their effectiveness increase. Noting that "in the Balkans life counts for nothing," the German army staff archivist Ernst Wisshaupt subsequently wrote: "Even with the *most unrestricted* reprisal measures—up until the end of August a total of approximately 1,000 communists *and Jews* had been shot or publicly hanged and the houses of the guilty burned down—it was not possible to restrain the continual growth of the armed revolt."[17] (Italics mine)

It was General Bader who analyzed the failure of all three German policies in the most unflinching terms. Reprisal policy only played into the hands of the Communists. Ambushed troops cried for revenge and shot people who were found in the fields. In most cases the guilty had long fled, the innocent suffered, and hitherto loyal Serbs went over to the partisans out of fear or bitterness.[18] The Serbian police were increasingly reproached for fighting against their countrymen and could no longer be relied upon. As for the German troops, no great success could be expected. Each division had only two regiments, no armored vehicles, and trucks so bad they could not leave the road. Individual battalions were as far as fifty or sixty kilometers apart, and so weakened by essential guard duty that only eighty or ninety men could be scraped together for pursuit commandos that were totally inadequate to cover the territory assigned. Quite simply, "The area is too great! The troops employed too weak!" (*Die Räume sind zu gross! Die eingesetzte Truppe zu schwach!*)[19]

Drastic measures were required, but the Germans in Belgrade and List in Greece advocated contrasting solutions based on starkly different interpretations of the nature of the partisan movement. Germans in Serbia emphasized two aspects of the insurgency. On the one hand, there were many causes for the inexorable growth of Serbian unrest. In addition to German reprisal policy, the feeling of Serbian national humiliation now compounded by the possible loss of the Banat to Hungary, the massive influx of penniless and maltreated Serbian refugees, the German toleration of Croatian atrocities, the high unemployment, food shortages, the long tradition of guerrilla resistance to foreign occupation, and a general sentiment of Slavic solidarity with Russia all created fertile soil for anti-German sentiment. On the other hand, however, these analyses noted that so far the Communists were the main force behind the insurgency. Though they draped their movement in nationalist garb, the Serbian nationalist circles, including the Chetniks, had hitherto remained aloof and deliberately avoided military confrontation with the Germans. The population at large still rejected communism, even if it did not cooperate with the German troops against the bands of insurgents.[20] It was of the utmost importance not to drive the Communists and Serbian nationalists into a united front; rather Germany must work with the latter against the former. Thus in late August, with the support of Turner, Benzler, Neuhausen, and Bader's chief of staff, Colonel Erich Kewisch, Danckelmann asked the former Serbian Minister of Defense, Milan Nedič, a popular figure untainted by corruption and a strong anti-Communist with a pro-German record, to become president of a new Serbian government replacing the now defunct provisional government. It was desperately hoped that Nedič would have the popularity and prestige to mobilize anti-Communist sentiment and win the support of wider circles of the Serbian population.[21]

The action was taken so precipitously that neither List nor higher officials in Berlin were consulted. List was not pleased. In addition to his pique over the *fait accompli* of the Germans in Belgrade, he disagreed with their basic assessment concerning the nature of the insurgent movement and the potential for Serbian collaboration. Though he reluctantly agreed to give the Nedič government a chance, he flatly rejected the local diagnosis of the insurgency, insisting that it was "not only a case of Communist, but of a general, national Serbian insurgent movement." He thus vehemently opposed reinforcing and improving the armament of the Serbian police or making use of Chetnik units to combat Communists.[22]

While requesting reinforcements from the OKW,[23] List made clear to the Germans in Belgrade that he preferred intensified military action and repression to greater reliance on Serbian collaborators. His chief of staff, Hermann Foertsch, had passed through Belgrade on September 1 and reported: "Downright violence still remains as the last resort."[24] List agreed. On September 4 he exhorted Danckelmann and Bader to ruthless action, and on the following day set forth specific guidelines for the suppression of the Serbian insurrection. These included "increased pressure on the population in areas where the insurgents are tolerated in order to bring the residents to the point where they will report the appearance of bands to the Germans" and "ruthless and immediate measures against the insurgents, against their accomplices and their families (hangings, burning down of villages involved, seizure of more hostages, deportation of relatives, etc., into concentration camps)." [*Rücksichtslose Sofortmassnahmen gegen die Aufständischen, deren Helfershelfer und ihre Angehörigen (Aufhängen, Niederbrennen beteiligter Ortschaften, vermehrte Festnahme von Geiseln, Abschieben der Familienangehörigen usw in Konzentrationslager.)*] Incompetent officers were to be removed, and if necessary brought to account.[25]

Why did Wilhelm List react in this way? He was neither a Nazi nor a traditional Prussian officer, but rather a widely read, cultured, deeply religious man trained at the military academy in Munich before World War I.[26] A great lover of classical music, especially Mozart, List reputedly never missed a performance of the opera while stationed in Vienna, and even received a rare "philharmonic ring" from the Vienna Philharmonic in recognition of his support.[27] In addition to his cultured tastes, List also had a reputation for discipline and order. In Poland he had ordered an end to shootings, rape, and burnings of synagogues,[28] and reputedly had had German soldiers shot for rape and jailed for plundering Jewish homes.[29] Commander of the Balkan campaign, List was a Grecophile who admired his defeated enemy. He left Archbishop Angelo Roncalli, the Papal nuncio in Istanbul and later Pope John XXIII, with the "best impression by the refinement and simplicity of his manners." Roncalli also noted List's severe discipline to protect Greek civilians from mistreatment by German soldiers and his efforts on behalf of food deliveries to Greece to avoid famine.[30] List was no mere careerist who would do anything to keep his position, nor a timid man afraid to stand up to Hitler. When ordered by Hitler to carry out an attack in the Caucasus in 1942 that List deemed suicidal for his troops, he refused, and his military career came to an abrupt end.[31]

In short, List's behavior vis-à-vis Serbia in September 1941 was not typical of the rest of his career nor of his character. Despite his claim at Nürnberg that the infamous September 5 guidelines must have been an OKW formulation that he had passed on without remembering them, they were his own.[32] They were not the reflection of OKW orders imposed from above nor of specifically Nazi convictions. Rather, they reflected the military frustrations of a professional soldier with little political sense. A strict disciplinarian with a paternalistic concern for the welfare of his own troops, List found the insurgency and its "insidious" methods an outrageous affront to his sense of order and decency. The insurgents and the unruly Serbian people from whom they sprang had to be punished. Whatever affection and respect List felt for the Greeks as a people of an ancient culture, he considered the Serbs in a quite different light. "They are far more passionate, hot blooded and more cruel" because of their history. "The individual in Serbia is obviously like every other peasant, under normal conditions, but as soon as differences arise, then caused by the hot blood in their veins, the cruelty caused by hundreds of years of Turkish domination errupts."[33] Because List had a stereotyped image of the Serbs, he felt they could be disciplined only with measures commensurate with their own violent nature. He had no patience for those like Turner, Benzler, and Danckelmann who wished to place greater reliance on Serbian collaboration.

List, and indeed almost every German officer in the Balkans, was tormented by another concern—the damage to the prestige and image of the German army caused by its inability to cope with the partisan tactics. This apprehension for the *Ansehen* of the German army is a recurring theme of the documents of this period. The partisan success was more than just an embarrassment to their professional pride. If not checked, the increasing display of German military impotence would hearten Germany's enemies and stimulate yet further resistance that could snowball into disaster.

In early September, when List fired off his exhortations for greater terror, this was no longer a fanciful prospect. The Chetniks were now entering the battle against the Germans, swept up in the wave of partisan success, and List's image of a national insurgency was becoming a self-fulfilling prophecy. In all of August the German Wehrmacht had suffered 30 dead, 23 wounded, and 1 missing in Serbia.[34] Suddenly, on the first of September, 100 men of a regional defense battalion were captured at Losnica, and three days later another 175 were captured in a breakout attempt from Krupanj.[35] Thus List was reacting to two major setbacks of unprecedented proportions in the guerrilla war which clearly demonstrated that the thinly stretched German troops in Serbia were not only impotent to suppress sabotage and ambush but were now threatened with piecemeal defeat and capture.

As the German position continued to deteriorate, even the proponents of the Nedič experiment admitted its failure, particularly when 450 Serbian police sent to Šabac refused to fight and Nedič himself confessed to Benzler that the only remaining solution was to crush the uprising with German forces alone.[36] List now moved to remedy what he considered the "intolerable chain of command" in Serbia, in which a "vain" and "superficial" Luftwaffe general, who had been seduced by the political calculations of Turner and Benzler, outranked the Wehrmacht troop commander. He proposed the unification of territorial and troop command under an "older, well-schooled general who has had front-line experience," and proposed 18th Corps commander General Franz Böhme as "especially suitable for this position."[37] Presumably Böhme, a general in the Austrian army before the Anschluss, would have few inhibitions about repression in Serbia.[38] List also reiterated his request for a front-line division. Both requests were quickly granted. The 342nd division was dispatched from France, and Böhme was appointed plenipotentiary commanding general in Serbia.[39]

Upon his arrival in Belgrade on September 18, Böhme found Turner and Bader's chief of staff, Kewisch, fervent converts to List's call for "increased pressure on the population." A major punitive expedition by the 342nd division was already being planned for the Sava Bend region around Šabac, a particularly dense area of partisan activity. Both Kewisch and Turner urged that not only the men but also the women and children be driven from the area to deprive the insurgents of their food supply. As Turner wrote, "The entire population had to be punished, not only the men" (*die Gesamtheit der Bevölkerung muss also gestraft werden, nicht nur die Männer)* for such "apparent" *(scheinbar)* cruelty was the only means to bring the people to their senses.[40]

Between September 22 and 25 Böhme issued his orders for the Sava Bend *Strafexpedition.*[41] The premise was that the population in its entirety had joined the insurgency. Through ruthless measures, a horrifying example had to be made that would become known throughout Serbia immediately. Men between fourteen and seventy years of age were to be placed in a concentration camp at Jarak near Mitrovica. The female population was to be driven off into the Cer mountains by every possible means. All inhabitants who participated in resistance or in whose houses ammunition or weapons were found or who attempted to flee were to be shot and their houses burned down. In a message to the troops, Boehme exhorted:

> Your mission lies in . . . the country in which German blood flowed in 1914 through the treachery of Serbs, men and women. You are avengers of these dead. An intimidating example must be created for the whole of Serbia, which must hit the whole population most severely. Anyone who wishes to rule charitably sins against the lives of his comrades. He will be called to account without regard for his person and placed before a court-martial.

> (Eure Aufgabe ist in einem Landstreifen durchzuführen, in dem 1914 Ströme deutschen Blutes durch die Hinterlist der Serben, Männer und Frauen, geflossen sind. Ihr seid Rächer dieser Toten. Es muss ein abschreckendes Beispeil für ganz Serbien geschaffen werden, dass die gesamte Bevölkerung auf das Schwerste treffen muss. Jeder, der Milde walten lässt, versündigt sich am Leben seiner Kameraden. Er wird ohne Rücksicht auf die person zur Verantwortung gezogen und vor ein Kriegsgericht gestellt.)

Ironically, just as the former champions of the Nedič experiment were now advocating draconian measures against the entire population to create "an intimidating example," Böhme was beginning to accept the view that the Nedič government and the Serbian police still had potential for the German cause, albeit in a secondary role. New reports began to reverse the negative picture of the Serbian police, and most importantly a major Chetnik leader in southern Serbia, Kosta Pečanac, broke with Mihailovič and openly allied with Nedič against the Communists.[42] Böhme concluded that Nedič had a following and was working for the German cause, and thus it was inexpedient to alienate him. Moreover, after a personal meeting, he came away impressed with Nedič as a "thoroughly honorable man." *(Der Minister erweckte den Eindruck eines durchaus ehrlichen Mannes.)*[43] On September 29 Böhme ordered that the rearming of the Serbian police be resumed.[44] Thus even as Böhme exhorted his men to be "avengers," he still held on to the prospect of using the Nedič government and its police. The Germans therefore could not be entirely oblivious to the political repercussions of their policy of exemplary terror.

On September 23, units of Lieutenant General Dr. Hinghofer's 342nd division marched into Šabac. The men of Sabac, as well as 1,100 Jewish refugees from central Europe interned there, were held for two days without food, force-marched to Jarak twenty-three kilometers away, and then marched back again four days later when the site proved unsuitable for a concentration camp.[45] Meanwhile, as the Germans fanned out from Šabac, particular towns were earmarked for total destruction and all suspected Communists were shot.[46] Then the fury began to subside. On October 2, Hinghofer ordered that the female population was not to be driven off into the mountains but left in the villages to take care of the cattle and the harvest.[47] Two days later Hinghofer ordered that shootings and burning of houses and villages be halted.[48] By then the 342nd division had gathered over 20,000 prisoners and executed 1,126.[49] Reluctant to release the male prisoners, Böhme requested their deportation to the Reich, but this was rejected by List.[50]

The 125th regiment, sent by List from Greece, carried out a similar punitive expedition to Valjevo south of Šabac. But despite these German offensives, Böhme continued to receive bad news. A company of regional defense troops was overpowered at Gorni Milanovac on September 29, though the death of ten men and the capture of sixty others was not confirmed until October 3. More shocking was the ambush on October 2 of a communications unit near Topola with the loss of twenty-one men. The German troops who surrendered were executed by machine-gun fire at close range.[51] Böhme's staff concluded that "the insurgent movement is still growing. No trace can be found of a deterrent effect from the clearing actions carried out until now by the 342nd division and the 125th regiment." *(Die Aufstandsbewegung noch immer im Wachsen ist. Von einer abschreckenden Wirkung der bis jetzt von 342 ID und IR 125 durchgeführten Säuberungsaktionen ist nichts zu verspüren.)*[52] Thus just as Hinghofer's punitive expedition in the Sava Bend was winding down—an action in which the attempt had still been made to separate Communist suspects from the rest of the population to avoid indiscriminate execution, and in which the interned Jews in Šabac had not been singled out for worse treatment—Böhme and his frustrated staff determined upon an even harsher policy.

On September 16 Keitel had issued a general directive to implement Hitler's demand for the "harshest measures" against communist insurgency in occupied territories. According to Keitel, all incidents, regardless of circumstances, implied communist origins. Because human life in the countries concerned often meant nothing and a deterrent effect could only be achieved through unusual harshness, Keitel ordered that 50 to 100 Communists were to be executed in retaliation for the death of each German soldier.[53] In the wake of the Topola ambush, Böhme's quartermaster, Captain Hans Georg Faulmüller, drafted a proposal, which was also initialed by Colonel Max Pemsel, the chief of staff: "As reprisal and expiation for every murdered German soldier, 100 Serbian prisoners are immediately to be shot. The chief of the Military Administration [Turner] is requested to select 2100 prisoners in the concentration camps Šabac and Belgrade (predominately Jews and Communists)." [*Als Repressalie und Sühne sind sofort für jeden ermordeten deutschen Soldaten 100 serbsiche Häftlinge zu erschiessen. Chef der Mil. Verwaltung wird gebeten, 2100 Häftlinge in den Konzentrationslagern Sabac und Belgrad (vorwiegend Juden und Kommunisten zu bestimmen).*] No written order was signed by Böhme; instead, the order was transmitted verbally by Faulmüller.[54]

On October 5, the day after his order for 2,100 reprisal executions, Böhme received a further communication from Keitel and a counterinsurgency directive from List as well. In his directive Keitel departed from his previous simplistic assertion that all resistance was communist in origin, and now required military commanders in occupied areas always to have on hand hostage pools of nationalists and middle-class democrats as well, so that in case of attack reprisal victims could be chosen appropriately.[55] List's directive was in response to Böhme's earlier request to deport to Germany all the interned Serbs at Šabac, for he opposed either holding them indefinitely or releasing them. List vetoed deportations and ordered that while those caught in battle were to be executed immediately, men merely encountered in the area of operations were to be investigated. Those proven to be partisans were to be executed, those suspected were to be held as hostages and shot in case of partisan activity in the area, and those not suspected of anti-German activity were to be released. Böhme's staff noted that List's directive was not entirely in accord with Keitel's earlier directive of September 16, which ordered the "harshest measures."[56] While in theory Keitel's and List's directives were not incompatible, in practice they would prove to be. Future events would show that if prisoners had to be investigated to spare the innocent, the ratio would be unobtainable; if the ratio was to be met, screening of prisoners would have to be dispensed with.

Böhme's staff proceeded to develop a general reprisal policy. Drafted by Faulmüller, initialed by Pemsel, and signed by Böhme, it was issued to all units on October 10, 1941:

> In Serbia it is necessary because of the "Balkan mentality" and the great expansion of the communist and nationalist-camouflaged insurgency movements, to carry out the orders of the OKW in the sharpest form. . . . In every command area in Serbia . . . all communists, all those suspected as such, *all Jews,* and a certain number of nationalist and democratically-inclined inhabitants are to be seized as hostages. (Italics mine)

> (In Serbien ist es auf Grund der "Balkanmentalität" und der grossen Ausdehnung kommunistischer und national getarnter Aufstandsbewegungen notwendig, die Befehle des OKW in schärfsten Form durchzuführen. . . . In allen Standorten in Serbien sind . . . umgehend alle Kommunisten, als solche verdächtigen männlichen Einwohner, sämtliche Juden, eine be-

stimmte Anzahl nationalistischer und demokratisch gesinnter Einwohner als Geiseln festzunehmen.)

One hundred hostages were to be shot for each German soldier or ethnic German killed and fifty for each wounded. The executions were to be carried out by army troops, preferably by the units suffering the losses.[57] This reprisal policy of Böhme, Pemsel, and Faulmüller was not simply a minimal compliance with the Keitel guidelines. Not only did they adopt the maximum suggested ratio of one hundred to one rather than the minimum of fifty to one, but they also explicitly included "all Jews," a group that Keitel had never mentioned. Why did they do this? The German military commanders in Serbia had long accepted the identification or at least the natural combination of Communist and Jew. The very first reprisal execution in late June had been carried out against "Communists and Jews," and by the end of the summer the military reported the reprisal execution of over one thousand "Communists and Jews." Böhme, Pemsel, and Faulmüller were not breaking new ground.

While many officers simply may have accepted the Communist-Jewish identification as an unquestioned and "self-evident" tenet of Nazi ideology, a narrowly professional and unideological mode of thinking among other officers led to the same results. It was obvious to every German officer that, given Nazi Germany's policies toward the Jews in occupied countries, they would assuredly be among Germany's enemies. As Field Marshal List stated at his trial: "I can well understand from the point of view of the Jews that they worked against the Germans and that they combined with the Communists. I say I can well understand that on the basis of events which had occurred."[58] Professional soldiers stood ready to defend their country against its enemies; they did not stand in judgment of or make their loyalty conditional upon the policies of their government that created those enemies. As long as the anti-Jewish measures in Serbia were perceived and construed as military measures against Germany's enemies, it did not require nazified zealots (though surely such were not lacking), merely conscientious and politically obtuse professional soldiers to carry them out.[59]

The inclusion of the Jews did not strike the Germans in Belgrade as extraordinary or unusual. On the contrary, it was a course of action that must have seemed almost natural and obvious. The male Jews of the Banat and Belgrade had been interned in the Belgrade concentration camp of Topovske Šupe in late August and September, and a large group of Jewish refugees from central Europe, primarily Austria, had been stranded in Yugoslavia when their travel arrangements to Palestine had collapsed, and had been interned in Šabac in June 1941.[60] Efforts by Foreign Office plenipotentiary Benzler, instigated by Turner, to deport the Jews to Rumania or elsewhere had been vetoed by the Foreign Office and the SS.[61] Thus the Jews remained in camps. Hinghofer and Böhme had also urged that the vast number of male prisoners rounded up in the Sava Bend be shipped to Germany, but List had vetoed this deportation and ordered the screening of prisoners and the holding of suspects as hostages. Böhme then ordered the erection of a large camp at Zasavica near Šabac for thirty thousand inmates.[62] Thus the German military in Serbia found themselves presiding over more and more camps, whose inmate population could not be deported and could only be decreased either by release, which they did not favor, or by hostage shooting.

The Serbian Jews constituted a group from whose ranks reprisal victims had already been selected for the past four months. Their continued internment and upkeep were no doubt viewed as a logistical burden. Their blanket identification by the Germans with the elusive communist enemy both obviated the need for the bothersome and unreliable screening process employed on Serbian prisoners and made them especially vulnerable and inviting targets for the venting of German frustrations. Under such circumstances it was almost inconceivable that the military authorities would have given the Jews a special protected status among the internees and not included them in the hostage pool.[63] As the Jews were already interned while the Communists for the most part defied capture, it had to be clear to Böhme and his staff upon whom the brunt of reprisal shootings would fall. The October 10 order all but sealed the fate of the male Serbian Jews before Wehrmacht firing squads.

In fact, the onslaught against the interned male Jews had already begun. On October 9 and 11 a firing squad from the communications unit which had suffered the casualties of the Topola ambush shot 449 Jews. Its commander, Lieutenant Walter Liepe, noted that the men returned from the first execution "satisfied" *(befriedigt)* but "unfortunately" *(leider)* his unit could not continue after the second day because of an assignment in the field. Other communications troops continued the executions in Belgrade thereafter. In Šabac the 342nd division had departed for an offensive in the Cer mountains, leaving the town and the Zasavica camp under army units borrowed from the 718th division in Croatia (parts of the 750th regiment under Major Faninger) and the 64th Reserve Police Battalion.[65] The records of neither unit have survived, but one witness, a Serb forced to dig graves and bury the corpses, lived to testify to the mass executions of the Šabac Jews and gypsies carried out by German soldiers at Zasavica on October 12 and 13, 1941.[66] This meant that in Šabac central European Jewish refugees, mostly Austrians, were shot by troops predominately of Austrian origin in retaliation for casualties inflicted by Serbian partisans on the German army!

On October 16 Turner proposed to Faulmüller the shooting of another 2,200 hostages for 10 German soldiers killed and 24 wounded in Valjevo. He offered to have the 64th Reserve Police Battalion shoot 600 and requested that the army provide firing squads for the other 1,600.[67] Three days later Pemsel assigned the task to the 734th regiment in Belgrade, so presumably he was fully aware that the incarcerated Jews in Belgrade were the intended victims.[68] Though determined as anyone to fulfill the quotas, Turner was alone among the Germans in Belgrade to show signs of ambivalence about using the interned Jews for this purpose. On October 17 he wrote his personal friend, SS-*Gruppenführer* Richard Hildebrandt, in Danzig:

> In the last eight days I had 2,000 Jews and 200 gypsies shot in accordance with the ratio 1:100 for bestially murdered German soldiers, and a further 2,200, likewise almost all Jews, will be shot in the next eight days. This is not a pretty business. At any rate, it has to be, if only to make clear what it means even to attack a German soldier, and, for the rest, the Jewish question solves itself most quickly in this way. Actually, it is false, if one is to be precise about it, that for murdered Germans—on whose account the ratio 1:100 should really be born by Serbs—100 Jews are shot instead; but the Jews we had in camps—after all, they too are Serb nationals, and besides, they have to disappear.[69]

> (Habe ich dann in den letzten 8 Tagen 2000 Juden und 200 Zigeuner erschiessen lassen nach der Quote 1:100 für bestialisch hingemordete deutsche Soldaten und weitere 2200, ebenfalls fast nur Juden, werden in den nächsten 8 Tagen erschossen. Eine schöne Arbeit ist das nicht! Aber immerhin muss es sein, um einmal den Leuten klar zu machen, was es heisst, einen deutschen Soldaten überhaupt nur anzugreifen und zum andern löst sich die Judenfrage auf die Weise am schnellsten. Es ist ja eigentlich falsch, wenn man es genau nimmt, das für ermordete Deutsche, bei denen ja das Verhältnis 1:100 zu Lasten der Serben gehen müsste, nun 100 Juden erschossen werden, aber die haben wir nun mal im Lager gehabt,—schliesslich sind es auch serbische StA und sie müssen ja auch verschwinden.)

If Turner was convinced that the Jews had to disappear, he was at least vaguely aware of the incongruity of shooting Jews in retaliation for the actions of Serbian partisans. Moreover, Turner's preferred solution for the disappearance of the Jews had been deportation to Rumania or elsewhere, and suddenly he saw the opportunity to press for this solution once more when Foreign Office Jewish expert Franz Rademacher and one of Eichmann's deputies, Friedrich Suhr, arrived in Belgrade on October 18.[70]

In September both Undersecretary Martin Luther in the Foreign Office and Reinhard Heydrich of the RSHA had been annoyed by Benzler's persistent requests (instigated by Turner) to deport the Serbian Jews. On October 4 Luther and Heydrich met and decided to send representatives to Belgrade to see if the Serbian Jewish question "could be settled on the spot" *(an Ort und Stelle erledigt werden könne).*[71] Upon arrival Rademacher and Suhr discovered that the desired local solution was already underway. When Rademacher met with Turner on October 19, however, the latter emphatically urged the deportation of the remaining two thousand male Jews interned in Belgrade. This was not a view shared by *Einsatzgruppe* leader Wilhelm Fuchs, who noted that the problem of the male Jews could be settled within a week by having them shot as hostages by the army. Already the number of incarcerated Jews did not suffice to fill the quota. On October 20 Fuchs, Turner, Rademacher, and Suhr met together. Faced with Rademacher's and Suhr's renewed veto of deportations, Turner raised no objection to Fuch's proposal to have the Jews shot within the framework of army reprisals. Rademacher reported: "The male Jews will be shot by the end of the week." *(Die männlichen Juden sind bis Ende dieser Woche erschossen.)*[72]

As the fate of the male Jews in Serbia was being sealed in Belgrade, events to the south of the capital in the towns of Kraljevo and Kragujevac were building to a crisis that would force the Germans to reappraise their reprisal policy. The 717th division of Major General Hoffman was responsible for this region, and the reprisal order of October 10 was to him a veritable hunting license. When units of his division suffered casualties in an attack on Kraljevo on October 15 and 16, they went on a house-to-house search through the city, and by the evening of the 17th had shot 1736 men and 19 "communist women."[73]

The Kraljevo massacre was shortly followed by an even larger one in Kragujevac, where Major König, a bitter critic of "soft" measures, was in command.[74] When German units returned from a punitive expedition to Gorni Milanovac with 133 hostages but 9 dead and 26 wounded of their own, Hoffmann ordered immediate retaliation. Sixty-six Communists and Jews and 53 prison inmates were seized, and König prepared to seize the remaining people to meet his quota of 2,300 from the population at large. The *Kreiskommandant,* Captain Bischofshausen, insisted that the population of the city had never caused a single German casualty. He urged that the reprisals be taken against the "communist-infested" *(kommunistisch verseucht)* villages in the area. König agreed, and on October 19 shot 245 men in Grosnica and 182 in Mackovac, which left the Germans still far short of their quota. Thus on the evening of October 19, König informed Bischofshausen of his intention to carry out the roundup of men in Kragujevac. On the following day 159 Communists, Jews, and prison inmates were shot, and 3,200 inhabitants of the city, including the students of the local high school, were seized. Mass shootings were carried out on October 21 until the quota of 2,300 had been met.[75]

List and Böhme had reaped the whirlwind sown by their constant incitements to "ruthless" terror. The two massacres at Kraljevo and Kragujevac had immediate repercussions, especially as the entire Serbian work force of an airplane factory in Kraljevo producing for the German war effort were among the victims. The OKW was dismayed at this incident.[76] Nedič also urged that the arbitrary shootings be stopped, and Böhme agreed.[77] Bader ordered all units to cease mass executions until further orders.[78] Meanwhile Faulmüller and Turner met several times to hammer out a new reprisal policy, which was forthcoming on October 25.[79]

> Arbitrary arrests and shootings of Serbs are driving to the insurgents circles of the population which up to now did not participate in the insurrection, strengthen the communist resistance, weaken the prospect of a quick suppression, and harm the ultimate political goal of the operation. The shooting of agents, Croats, and the entire personnel of German armaments factories are irreparable errors. In doubtful cases, the decision of superior authorities is to be attained.

> (Wahllose Festnahmen und Erschiessungen von Serben treiben am Aufstand bisher unbeteiligte Kreise der Bevölkerung zu den Aufständischen, stärken die Widerstandskraft des Kommunismus, schwächen die Aussichten auf schnelle Niederwerfung und schaden dem politischen Endziel des Einsatzes. Die Erschiessung von V-Leuten, Kroaten und ganzen Belegschaften deutschen Rüstungsbetriebe sind nicht wieder gutzumachende Fehlgriffe. In Zweifelsfällen ist vor der Erschiessung die Entscheidung der vorgesetzten Dienststelle einzuholen.)

Hostages were to be taken in sufficient numbers from the villages that were known as focal points of the insurgency, and the local *Feldkommandanturen* and *Kreiskommandanturen* were to be consulted. "It must thus be avoided, that precisely those elements of the population are seized and shot as hostages who, being nonparticipants in the insurrection, did not flee before the German punitive expedition." *(Dabei ist zu vermeiden, dass gerade der Rest der Bevölkerung als Geiseln festgenommen und erschossen wird, der—am Aufstand unbeteiligt—vor einer deutschen Strafexpedition nicht geflohen ist.)*

If the massacres at Kraljevo and Kragujevac moved Böhme to ensure that further arbitrary shootings of Serbs did not occur, that was of no help to the incarcerated Jews. If the Germans could conceive that not all Serbs were Communists and that the random shooting of innocent Serbs would damage German interests, they had no doubt that all Jews were anti-German. And if more care had to be exercised in selecting Serbian hostages, the pressure to find hostages elsewhere was that much greater. Moreover, past experience demonstrated that their elimination involved no political cost, for in contrast to Kraljevo and Kragujevac, no one had protested the Belgrade and Šabac *Judenerschiessungen*. Harald Turner, who had previously sought to deport Jews, best exemplified this attitude in a memorandum of October 26.[80] On the one hand he noted that "the belief in the feeling for justice of the German Wehrmacht must be destroyed if not only people who are *completely* innocent are shot to death but—as occurred in one case—just those men of the village were executed who remained at the place of work waiting for German troops, because of their confidence in their own innocence." *(Der Glaube an den Rechtsgefuehl der deutschen Wehrmacht vernichtet werden muss, wenn nicht nur völlig Unschuldige erschossen werden, sondern—wie es in einem Fall sich ereignet hat—gerade diejenigen Männer in einer Ortschaft exekutiert werden, die im Vertrauen auf ihre Unschuld . . . an ihren Arbeitsstätte die deutschen Truppen erwarteten.)* On the other hand he noted: "As a matter of principle it must be said that the Jews and gypsies in general represent an element of insecurity and thus a danger to public order and safety. . . . That is why it is a matter of principle in each case to put all Jewish men and all male gypsies at the disposal of the troops as hostages." *(Grundsätzlich ist festzulegen, dass Juden und Zigeuner ganz allgemein ein Element der Unsicherheit und damit Gefährdung der öffentlichen Ordnung und Sicherheit darstellt. . . . Es sind deshalb grundsätzlich in jedem Fall alle jüdischen Männer und alle männlichen Zigeuner als Geiseln der Truppe zur Verfügung zu stellen.)*

The murder of the remaining 2,000 male Jews in Serbia began on October 27.[81] Two days later 250 gypsies were arrested in Belgrade to swell the hostage pool.[82] The shooting commando of Lieutenant Hans-Dietrich Walther resumed the executions on October 30. Walther noted in his summary report over "the shooting of Jews and gypsies":

> At first my soldiers were not impressed. On the second day, however, it became obvious that one or another did not have the nerve to carry out shootings over a long period of time. It is my personal impression that during the shooting one does not have psychological blocks. They set in, however, after several days one reflects about it on evenings alone.
>
> (Anfangs waren meine Soldaten nicht beeindruckt. Am 2. Tage jedoch machte sich schon bemarkbar, dass der eine oder andere nicht die Nerven besitzt, auf längere Zeit eine Erschiessung durchzuführen. Mein persön-licher Eindruck ist, dass man während der Erschiessung keine seelischen Hemmungen bekommt. Diese stellen sich jedoch ein, wenn man nach Tagen abends in Ruhe darüber nachdenkt.)

A week later, after Walther had had some days to reflect, he was ordered to carry out yet a third execution. Afterward he went to his battalion commander and pleaded release from his assignment, because his nerves were finished and he dreamed of the shootings at night. The next execution was given to a different company commander. Presumably, the 64th Reserve Police Battalion also shot its six hundred hostages, as promised by Turner.[83]

By the end of October, as the second and final round of *Judenerschies-sungen* was underway, the tide of battle in Serbia had definitely turned in favor of the Germans. German assessments noted the breaking up of the insurgent movement, the flight of the Communists to Croatia, the turn-about of the Chetniks, who now began to fight the Communists and to ask the Germans for arms, and the increasingly effective and reliable perform-ance of the Serbian police.[84] The Germans were quite convinced that their

General Feldmarschall Wilhelm List, Military Commander Southeast. Sentenced to life; released on medical parole, 1951.
—*Bundesarchiv Koblenz, 77/121/22A*

SS-Standartenführer Dr. Wilhelm Fuchs, commander, Sipo-SD Einsatzgruppe, Serbia. Executed, 1946.
—*Berlin Document Center*

General Franz Böhme, Plenipotentiary Commanding General, Serbia. Committed suicide after Nuremberg indictment.
—*Bundesarchiv Koblenz, 79/113/2*

Untersturm-führer Harry Wentritt, chief mechanic, Security Police garage, Berlin. Three-year sentence.

SS-Sturmbann-führer Bruno Sattler, head of Gestapo for Jewish affairs and the Semlin camp, Security Police, Serbia.
—*Berlin Document Center*

SS-Obersturmbannführer Walter Rauff, head, technical affairs bureau, Reich Main Security Office, Berlin. Escaped to Chile; died there, 1984.
—*Berlin Document Center*

SS-Hauptsturmführer and Police Major Friedrich Pradel, head of automotive section, Security Police, Reich Main Security Office, Berlin.
—*Berlin Document Center*

SS-Standartenführer Emmanuel Schäfer, chief of Security Police, Serbia. One year and nine months denazification sentence; six years and six months criminal court sentence.
—*Berlin Document Center*

Assembly of the Zrenjanin Jews in the Banat, after the arrival of
the Germans in the spring of 1941.
—*Jewish History Museum, Belgrade*

Deportation of the Zrenjanin
Jews from the Banat to Belgrade, summer of 1941 (2 pictures).
—*Jewish History Museum, Belgrade*

Round-up of civilian population at Sabac, September 1941
—*Staatsarchiv Nürnberg, KV-Anklage, Dokumente, Fotokopien, J-71*

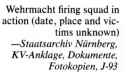

Wehrmacht firing squad in action (date, place and victims unknown)
—*Staatsarchiv Nürnberg, KV-Anklage, Dokumente, Fotokopien, J-93*

Gas Van (2 pictures), taken by Polish photographer after the liberation.
—*Yad Vashem Archives*

Semlin Exposition Grounds across the Sava River from Belgrade, subsequently converted into the Judenlager.
—*Jewish History Museum, Belgrade*

Pavilion of the Semlin Exposition Grounds, used as a prisoners' barracks.
—*Jewish History Museum, Belgrade*

Entry gate to the Semlin camp (through which prisoners may have walked before being loaded into the gas van).
—*Jewish History Museum, Belgrade*

reprisal measures had made a major contribution to their success.[85] Yet the reprisal quotas were no longer enforced with the earlier severity and exactness. For instance, the 342nd division reported a shortfall of 3250 reprisal executions on both October 30 and November 11, stating that they had no prisoners available.[86] Though 1345 reprisal shootings were carried out in November and an additional 984 in December, this still left the Germans far behind in fulfilling the quota.[87] With random reprisals excluded and the supply of Jews exhausted, the quotas simply could not be met. When General Bader replaced Böhme on December 5, he had a statistical study prepared of the reprisal program. It concluded that at least 11,164 reprisal shootings had been carried out as of December 5, 1941, though this figure was admittedly too low, for the compilers of the report had not received data from the 718th division (which had carried out the Šabac shootings in mid-October) and several other units. Calculating German casualties and adjusting for partisans reported killed in battle, the report concluded that there was still a staggering shortfall of 20,174 reprisals.[88]

On December 22 Bader issued a lowered reprisal quota, stipulating ratios of fifty and twenty-five to one, for dead and wounded respectively.[89] But still to be taken as reprisal prisoners were those who "because of their attitude and behavior were earmarked to atone for German lives, for example, Communists captured without weapons, gypsies, Jews, criminals, and so forth" *(auf Grund ihrer Einstellung und ihres Verhaltens zur Sühne für deutsche Menschenleben bestimmt sind, z.B. nicht mit der Waffe betroffene Kommunisten, Zigeuner, Juden, Verbrecher u. dergl.).*[90] Even after the male Jews had been murdered, the Germans could not refrain from counting them as a group who, because of their presumed attitude and behavior, could be automatically counted as reprisal prisoners doomed to death. Thus if the Germans did not fulfill their reprisal quota, it was because insufficient numbers of Communists could be found, the political cost of randomly killing Serbs was too high, and the supply of "expendable" Jews and gypsies was exhausted. There is very little reason to believe the quota would not have been met if enough Jews had been available.

In conclusion, the mass murder of the male Jews in Serbia was primarily accomplished by the German Wehrmacht, though it certainly received willing help from the Security and Order Police of the SS. This mass murder was the culmination of a process in which the German occupation authorities had first singled the Jews out for special persecution in the spring of 1941 and subjected them to disproportionate reprisals and internment in the summer. Once the partisan resistance drove the Germans to inflict upon themselves the obligation to fulfill the maximum reprisal quota, all interned Serbs were at high risk, but the interned male Jews were doomed. The German military could conceive of innocent Serbs but not innocent Jews. They accepted the fact that not all Serbs were Communists, and thus perceived the political expediency of screening Serbian prisoners and releasing those beyond suspicion, especially after the catastrophe of the Kraljevo and Kragujevac massacres. But it was axiomatic that all Jews were anti-German and thus a legitimate target of a professional organization dedicated to defending Germany against its enemies. They were moreover an expendable group whose elimination entailed no politically disadvantageous repercussions. The local SS forces, Fuchs and belatedly Turner, and Berlin, through its traveling representatives Rademacher and Suhr, may have given an additional push in late October to finish the job. But they were pushing on an open door. The policy of killing all the adult male Jews in Serbia as hostages had been articulated by Böhme, Pemsel, and Faulmüller already in early October and was reaffirmed in principle by Bader in late December. Thus a commonality of interest had emerged between the Wehrmacht, SS, and Foreign Office to kill these Jews even before the Final Solution to murder all the Jews of Europe was in operation. When such events could happen, it is no wonder that, when instituted, the European-wide genocide program met with no meaningful resistance from any organized segment of German society, and certainly not from the Wehrmacht.

3

The Development and Production
of the Nazi Gas Van

The development and production of the gas van constituted an intermediate stage between the mobile firing squad procedures of the *Einsatzgruppen* in Russia and the stationary gas chambers of the death camps
in Poland in the Nazi attempt to murder the European Jews. The ancestry
of the gas van, in both technology and personnel, traced back to the
euthanasia program aimed at mentally and hereditarily ill Germans that
had been ordered by Hitler in 1939. The motive behind developing the gas
van sprang from the desire to alleviate the psychological burden upon the
firing-squad murderers, many of them middle-aged family men who were
disturbed most of all by the endless shooting of women and children. And
the most effective use of the gas van was in stationary camp settings—
above all, Chelmno (Kulmhof) in the Warthegau but also Semlin near
Belgrade and Trostinez near Minsk—presaging the more sophisticated
factories of assembly-line murder at the major death camps such as Treblinka and Auschwitz.

Though the gas van was in retrospect a temporary solution to some of
the technological and psychological problems facing the Germans in carrying out the Final Solution, it was not an insignificant episode. The fall of
1941 and the spring of 1942, when the gas van was being developed and
produced, spanned a crucial period in the evolution of Nazi Jewish policy
when systematic mass murder of Jews outside Russia was just getting
underway. The relative degree of continuity or discontinuity between the
Einsatzgruppen operations in Russia and the subsequent mass murder of
European Jews on the one hand, and of centralized and conscious policy
implementation or spontaneous local improvisation on the other, has been
a matter of some debate.[1] In this regard the history of the gas van reveals
at least some continuity between the *Einsatzgruppen* operations and the

subsequent attempt to extend the Final Solution to the rest of the European Jews, and rather extensive coordination by central authorities in Berlin of events occurring in various parts of Europe during this crucial period, which offers little comfort to the advocates of the "discontinuity" and "improvisation" theories.

Moreover, the history of the gas van provides a glimpse into the day-to-day activities and reactions of the lower-echelon perpetrators of the Final Solution. Various types of specialists—in this case, scientists and automotive technicians—adapted both their talents and psyches to the new task at hand. The defense mechanisms they developed and the zeal they displayed illustrate once again the ease with which careerism can be exploited to harness ordinary people in the service of mass murder.

As in the case of the stationary gas chambers, the first Nazi experiments with gas vans took place as part of the euthanasia program. Following the outbreak of war in September 1939, Hitler had instigated the systematic killing of "unworthy" life.[2] Though the program was administered by Philippe Bouhler and Victor Brack in the Fuehrer's Chancellory, it involved considerable participation by the SS. Many of the personnel of the six euthanasia institutes or killing centers were SS men who would subsequently serve in the Polish death camps of Belzec, Sobibor, and Treblinka.[3] Moreover, advice on killing methods was sought from the crime laboratory of the *Kriminaltechnische Institut* (KTI or Criminal Technical Institute). The KTI of Dr. Walter Heess was a component of the Criminal Police (Kripo) of Artur Nebe, which in turn was lodged within the Reich Security Main Office (*Reichssicherheitshauptamt* or RSHA) of Himmler's deputy, Reinhard Heydrich. Heess was a longtime chemist with the Stuttgart police who joined the party in May 1933. He was called to Berlin in April 1938 to head the KTI and was taken into the SS in 1939. The toxicology expert and head of the chemical section of the KTI's crime laboratory was a young protégé of Heess, Dr. Albert Widmann. Born in 1912 the son of a locomotive engineer, Widmann was a self-made man. He got his doctorate in chemistry from the *Technische Hochschule* in Stuttgart in 1938, where he had also worked for Dr. Heess during vacations. When Heess went to Berlin in 1938, he brought Widmann with him. Though a member of the National Socialist Motor Corps (NSKK) since the summer of 1933, Widmann did not attain party membership until May 1937 and only entered the SS in December 1939. Informed by Nebe of the euthanasia program and the advisory function of the KTI, Widmann performed various tests on animals and then proposed chemically pure carbon monoxide gas as the killing agent. Attracted by tasks "more important to the war effort" *(kriegswichtiger)* then fighting crime, Widmann would subsequently become involved not only in the gas van but also in demolition, poison gas grenades, and poison bullets.[4] Distribution of the bottled carbon monoxide was handled by another SS chemist, *Untersturmführer* Dr. August Becker. Born in 1900, he served briefly in

World War I and attained his doctorate from the University of Giessen in 1933. In contrast to Widmann, Becker ranked as an *Altkämpfer,* having joined the NSDAP in 1930 and the SS in 1931. A scientific assistant to the Gestapo in Giessen since 1934, Becker was brought to Berlin in 1938 and "loaned" to Brack in January 1940 to help with the euthanasia program.[5] Subsequently he procured steel bottles of CO from the chemical firm of Badischer Anilin- und Sodafabrik (BASF) in Ludwigshafen and delivered them to the killing centers. Apparently both Widmann and Becker each personally carried out several of the initial gassings to test the method and instruct the personnel.[6]

With the euthanasia program underway in Germany, the mental hospitals of East Prussia and the incorporated territories were not spared. However, the procedure was different there. Instead of the victims being sent to one of the six institutes equipped with stationary gas chambers, the killing was done by a *Sonderkommando* under *Hauptsturmführer,* Herbert Lange, stationed in Posen.[7] Lange's unit made frequent trips from Posen to the Wartheland and East and West Prussia to "evacuate" inmates from mental institutions. Usually Lange arrived with a list of patients, without relatives or deemed incurable, who were taken off without medical files or personal belongings in a large Kaiser's Coffee truck at roughly three-hour intervals and never seen again. In fact, the victims were gassed, as chemically pure carbon monoxide stored in the driver's compartment was released from steel bottles through a hose leading into a specially constructed airtight compartment in which the victims were locked.[8] In one exceptionally large killing operation, 1,558 patients from East Prussian hospitals were assembled at the Soldau transit camp in May 1940 and killed by Lange's *Sonderkommando* over a two-week period.[9]

Thus the connection between Nebe and his crime lab scientists, Brack's euthanasia program, and Lange's *Sonderkommando* using airtight trucks as mobile gas chambers was established long before the question of gassing Jews had arisen. When the possibility was first weighed of using gas to kill Jews in Russia, for which the supply of bottled carbon monoxide was inadequate, the idea of using motor exhaust stemmed not from local improvisation by Lange in Posen but once again from the scientists in Berlin. The impetus to use gas to kill the Jews was provided by the obvious deficiencies in the *Einsatzgruppen* method of mass shootings. There were many complaints about the psychological burden upon the executioners. After a shaken Himmler had witnessed a mass shooting, he ordered Nebe, who was also chief of *Einsatzgruppe* B, to ascertain whether better results could not be obtained with explosives or poison gas. In fact, within the KTI Heess had already mentioned to Widmann, while riding home from work on the underground (between Wittenberg-Platz and Thiel-Platz, Widmann remembered exactly), that Nebe had suggested the possibility of using exhaust gas instead of bottled gas. The suggestion had been occasioned by Nebe's close brush with death, when, returning home from a party after drinking heavily, he had fallen asleep in his garage with the car engine running. Discussion of killing through exhaust gas was not limited to an informal chat on the underground, as several witnesses remembered hearing the possibility bandied about at the KTI. In September 1941 Widmann and the KTI's explosives expert were summoned to Nebe in Minsk. An explosives test proved most unsatisfactory; it required two explosions to kill all the test victims, a group of mental patients locked in a bunker, and left parts of bodies strewn about and even hanging from nearby trees. The gassing test was more successful; five mental patients were killed in a sealed room by introducing exhaust gas through a hose from a car and truck parked outside.[10]

The two threads of Lange's mobile gas vans and Nebe's tests with exhaust gas came together in the hands of Reinhard Heydrich, head of both the RSHA and the *Einsatzgruppen.* To design and produce a gas van using motor exhaust, he turned to the head of his office for technical affairs (Amt II D), Walter Rauff. Born in 1906, Rauff had been, like Heydrich, a professional naval officer until personal problems (a messy divorce) dimmed his career prospects. Within two months of his divorce, Rauff resigned from the service and, though a party member for less than a year, was immediately taken into the SD and rapidly promoted. Rauff credited his contact with Heydrich to SA-*Obergruppenführer* Dietrich von Jagow, who had had naval reserve training on Rauff's ship. Rauff's recruitment to the SS was so eagerly desired that even his "urgent" remarriage to a woman whose former husband was Jewish was personally allowed by Himmler without damage to his new career. Rauff repaid his new benefactors with a zeal that always earned the highest accolades in his personnel file.[11]

Rauff's jurisdiction included all motor vehicles—some four thousand—of the Security Police, which were under the direct supervision of Friedrich Pradel. Pradel was born in 1901, attained his *Abitur,* and briefly attended university before taking a three-year training course as a salesman. In 1925 he began officer training in the Prussian *Schutzpolizei* (Protective Police or Schupo) and made a successful career specializing in automotive affairs. In 1937 he was brought to the main office of the Order Police *(Ordnungspolizei Hauptamt)* in Berlin by its chief, Kurt Daluege, but then was placed in charge of motor vehicles within the Security Police main office. In 1938 he was granted SS rank corresponding to his Schupo rank and entered the NSDAP with membership retroactive to 1937. It was not until February 1942 that Pradel requested official transfer from the Schupo to the Security Police. Rauff then noted his lack of leadership qualities, had nothing to say of his "inner attitude" or "Weltanschauung," but conceded that Pradel took care of his vehicles "with considerable success" and that there was no prospect that the Security Police could procure a cadre of motor vehicle leaders of its own in the future. He thus supported the transfer request, which was not granted until December

1943. In 1944 Pradel and several of his co-workers were arrested on suspicion of trading benzin for liquor on the black market. Pradel was sent to the concentration camp at Orienburg but released in January 1945 for duty in a Waffen-SS unit.[12] Thus Pradel fell far short of the Nazi ideal but was useful for his technical expertise until he succumbed to the temptation of corruption.

Pradel's chief mechanic and head of the Security Police motor pool garage on the Prinz Albrecht Strasse was Harry Wentritt. Born in 1903, the son of a Berlin trolley driver, he began vocational training as an electrical mechanic at the age of sixteen. Wentritt joined the NSDAP and a SA-*Motorsturm* of the NSKK in 1932. He was hired by the Gestapo as an auto welder in 1935. In 1936 he transferred from the NSKK to the SS, and in June 1941 he became head of the Berlin garage.[13]

In September 1941, presumably after Nebe reported the results of Widmann's test, Rauff summoned Pradel to his office. At that time Pradel had already organized the motor pools of the *Einsatzgruppen* while they were at their training camp at Pretzsch, had become aware of complaints of drivers who had been impressed into service during mass executions of Jews, and had been on the distribution list of at least four daily situation reports of the *Einsatzgruppen* in early August, which mentioned many executions of Jews and noted on August 10 that *Einsatzgruppe* A had liquidated a total of twenty-nine thousand "persons."[14] Pradel was not, therefore, unaware of events in Russia.

Rauff instructed Pradel to ask his chief mechanic, Wentritt, if exhaust gas could be directed into a closed truck to kill the passengers. A "more humane method of execution" was needed for the *Einsatzgruppen* in Russia, Rauff noted. Though Rauff did not mention Jews, it was clear to Pradel who were the intended victims.[15] Pradel then put the question to Wentritt, explaining that the firing squads in Russia suffered frequent nervous breakdowns and needed a "more humane" method of killing. Pradel informed him that the work would have to be done in Wentritt's garage. Wentritt asked Pradel if there was a way out, but Pradel told him—"in a friendly tone"—to think of his wife and children. The mechanic confirmed that the proposed alterations were technically quite simple. Wentritt too had heard of mass shootings of Jews in Russia. Though admittedly not endowed with a quick mind, in the course of time he too realized that the proposed gas vans were for killing Jews.[16]

When Pradel relayed Wentritt's affirmative answer, Rauff instructed him to contact Dr. Heess of the KTI, who explained how the gas van should function. Pradel had the impression that a gas van of this design did not yet exist. Rauff instructed Pradel to procure suitable trucks, but the latter was unsuccessful. Rauff then managed to secure five Saurer-model chassis himself.[17] Pradel and Wentritt visited the body-making firm of Gaubschat, where Pradel explained that the RSHA needed closed trucks to transport contagious corpses in the occupied territories. When agreement was reached on the conversion work to be performed by Firma Gaubschat, the first Saurer chassis was delivered to them.[18] Wentritt then brought the converted Saurer, which now looked like a furniture van with a storage compartment about five meters long and two meters wide and painted field gray, to his workshop. He inserted a T-joint in the exhaust pipe and bored a two-inch hole in the floor of the rear compartment. A perforated U-shaped pipe was welded on the inside and a nozzle at the outside of the hole. The T-joint and nozzle could be connected by a pipe, and the regular exhaust pipe could be capped.[19] When the work was done, Wentritt drove the prototype to the KTI for testing.

Upon Wentritt's arrival in the courtyard of the KTI, Widmann summoned his young chemists to the closed box-type truck and explained that through adjusting the timing of the ignition, one could maximize the amount of poisonous carbon monoxide in the exhaust. He also explained how to measure the carbon monoxide content within the sealed rear compartment after the exhaust gas was directed therein. One of his men donned a gas mask and conducted the measurement. With this truck, Widmann explained, the firing squads on the eastern front would be spared.[20]

Some days later, in October or possibly early November, Dr. Heess drove two of the young chemists who had been present at the recent carbon monoxide measurement to the concentration camp at Sachsenhausen. There they found the gas van admidst a group of about thirty SS-officers. Forty naked Russians were led from a nearby barrack and locked in the truck, which drove to the crematorium in another part of camp. The observers followed on foot and caught up with the truck some five or ten minutes later. The motor was still running, and groaning and banging against the inside could still be heard. After twenty minutes a check through a peep hole from the driver's cab confirmed that all were dead. Many of the bodies, pressed against the door, tumbled out when the truck was opened. Prisoners unloaded the rest. The pink color of the bodies indicated that death had been caused by poisoning, not suffocation, and Heess and the SS-officers deemed the test a success.[21]

Despite the difficulty in procuring truck chassis, production of the gas vans now moved forward. Firma Gaubschat was contracted for a total of thirty conversions.[22] In addition to the large Saurer type, a smaller Opel-Blitz or Diamond model was converted as well. The former was to hold approximately fifty people, the latter twenty-five to thirty. Each truck took eight to fourteen days from the time of initial delivery to Firma Gaubschat until Wentritt had completed his final modifications. Because of the size of his workshop, Wentritt could work on only one truck at a time.[23]

In addition to the Saurer and Opel-Blitz models, two Dodge trucks were also converted into gas vans in the fall of 1941. Herbert Lange's *Sonderkommando* had moved from Posen and set up a permanent base in

Chelmno in November 1941, directly after Lange returned from a trip to Berlin. The *Sonderkommando* began gassing Jews on December 8, after the arrival of two Dodge gas vans with drivers. A Saurer from Berlin arrived in Chelmno only later. The origin of these two Dodge gas vans is not known for certain. However, it is most probable that they were part of Rauff's RSHA production process, for the design of the airtight compartment and the exhaust gas hookup were identical to those of the other gas vans, and at least one of the Chelmno drivers was dispatched through the Berlin motor pool in the same way as the drivers sent to the *Einsatzgruppen*.[24] If the *Sonderkommando* Lange was the first into action with the gas vans, the *Einsatzgruppen* did not have long to wait. *Einsatzkommando 5* of *Einsatzgruppe C* in Kiev received its first gas vans shortly before Christmas, and the others began receiving theirs after the New Year.[25]

Procurement remained a constant problem, and initially demand exceeded supply. In late October 1941 Victor Brack advised the *Reichskommissariat* Ostland that a sufficient supply of gassing apparatus *(Vergasungsapparate)* was not at hand in Berlin and production faced much greater difficulty in the Reich than it would locally in the Ostland. He offered to send yet another chemist, Dr. Helmut Kallmeyer, to provide expertise on the spot, an offer that was apparently not accepted.[26] When the head doctor at Mauthausen also requested a gas van in the spring of 1942, Rauff could not help. All gas vans were already in use; more were on order, but he could not say when the chassis, in short supply, would be made available. As he assumed that Mauthausen could not wait indefinitely, he suggested that the KTI supply it with bottled carbon monoxide or other "means of help." *(Hilfsmitteln)*[27]

To supervise and report on the gas-van operations already in the field, Rauff sent SS-*Untersturmführer* Dr. August Becker to visit all the *Einsatzgruppen*. On loan from the RSHA to the euthanasia program since January 1940 in order to deliver bottled gas to the institutes, Becker was reclaimed by Himmler from Brack now that the euthanasia program was winding down. "Himmler wanted to use the people released from euthanasia who were experts in gassing, such as myself, in the great gassing program getting underway in the east," Becker frankly admitted. *(Himmler wollte die bei der Euthanasie freiwerdenen Leute, die Fachleute in der Vergassung waren wie ich, für die gross anlaufende Vergasungsaktion im Osten einsetzen.)* Becker, whose work in euthanasia was deemed "especially deserving" *(hat sich . . . besondere Verdienste erworben)*, was sent to Rauff in early December; after a delay due to an automobile accident, Becker reached *Einsatzgruppe D*, his first stop, in late January 1942, and gradually worked his way north to Riga.[28] While waiting for more truck chassis, and with orders for ten of the thirty conversions already contracted with Gaubschat still unfilled, Rauff's men could turn their attention to making technical improvements based upon Becker's and others' reports.

Unloading the van was a constant source of complaint. To make it as quick and automatic as possible, Pradel proposed on April 24, 1942, that in the new vans a second wooden grill floor be placed on rollers, so it could slide out. Rauff approved, but Firma Gaubschat replied that the desired change could not be carried out in the foreseeable future because so many of their technical personnel had been drafted. Furthermore, the winch needed to pull the grill could not be procured for from ten to twelve months.[29]

Becker reported further difficulties in mid-May. The large Saurer trucks were not suited to cross-country driving and could not reach the burial sites except in very dry weather. The breaks required frequent repairs. The bumpy terrain had loosened seals and rivets, so that many trucks were no longer airtight. The vans had become so well known that the civilian population openly referred to them as the "death trucks." *(Todeswagen)* Though he had had windows painted on the sides, Becker did not think the disguise would be effective for very long. Because the engines were often run too fast, the exhaust gas was too impure, and the victims were suffocated painfully instead of being "peacefully put to sleep" *(friedlich einschlafen);* the result was ghastly—horribly distorted faces and bodies covered with excrement and vomit. For security reasons the *Einsatzgruppen* commanders made their own men unload the vans, and they complained of headaches after each unloading operation. In most units the men preferred shooting.[30]

An incident even more embarrassing than this litany of shortcomings in the gas van occurred when the Saurer truck sent to Chelmno exploded. When the truck started, the back doors blew open and the Jews, some of them burned, came out.[31] This was judged an isolated case caused by operator error, the automotive experts in Pradel's unit decided, because otherwise "ninety-seven thousand had been processed since December 1941 with three trucks in action without any defects in the vehicles being encountered." *(Seit Dezember 1941 wurden . . . mit 3 eingesetzten Wagen 97.000 verarbeitet, ohne dass Mängel an den Fahrzeugen auftraten.)*[32]

The zealous men of Pradel's unit did search for remedies to other shortcomings of the gas van, however. In a "single-copy" memo astonishing for its euphemisms even by Nazi standards, dispatcher Willy Just[33] suggested shortening the last ten Saurer trucks still to be delivered. They could not negotiate the Russian terrain fully loaded, and thus too much empty space existed to be filled with carbon monoxide, and the operating time was greatly lengthened. A shorter, fully loaded truck could operate much more quickly. A shortening of the rear compartment would not disadvantageously affect the weight balance, overburdening the front axle, because: "Actually a compensation in the weight distribution takes place automatically through the fact that the cargo in the struggle toward the back door during the operation always is preponderately located there." *(Tatsächlich findet aber ungewollt ein Ausgleich in der*

Gewichtsverteilung dadurch statt, dass das Ladegut beim Betrieb in dem Streben nach der hinteren Tür immer vorwiegend dort liegt.) Because the connecting pipe was quickly rusted through by "fluids," the gas should be introduced from above, not below. To facilitate cleaning, an eight- to twelve-inch hole should be made in the floor and provided with a cover opened from the outside. The floor should be slightly inclined, and the cover equipped with a small sieve. Thus all "fluids" would flow to the middle, the "thin fluids" would exit even during the operation, and "thicker filth" *(dicker Schmutz)* could be hosed out afterward. Just also repeated the proposal for a sliding floor grill. He suggested the Firma Sodomka in Hohenmauth in the Protectorate for the job, and Rauff approved.[34]

Firma Sodomka was rejected, however. In the wake of the Heydrich assassination, a Czech firm with Czech workers was deemed unsuitable for security reasons. Pradel turned again to Firma Gaubschat in late June, with the request to construct a prototype incorporating the new features, but Firma Gaubschat was not ready to resume further conversion work until late September.[35] There is no evidence that any of the last ten gas vans of the thirty ordered in late 1941 was in fact built thereafter.

The gas van remained a technological curiosity of the Final Solution for two reasons. First, it failed to perform satisfactorily the function for which it was initially designed—to provide a "more humane" method of killing. This was not for the sake of the victims, of course, but to lighten the psychological burden on the killers. Exhaust gas, in contrast to the chemically pure carbon monoxide used in the euthanasia institutes, caused the victims such agony that the task of unloading the vans proved far more burdensome than shooting the victims. The hardened executioners of the *Einsatzgruppen* thus preferred to retain their older methods, and little use was made of the vans by the mobile killing units.

The gas vans proved successful to the executioners only when incorporated into a stationary camp setting, such as at Chelmno, where non-German labor could be kept on hand for unloading without threatening security or secrecy, and the trucks were not faced with driving over difficult terrain. More than 152,000 Jews were ultimately killed in the Chelmno gas vans.[36] Outside Chelmno continuous use of the gas van occurred in at least two places. At the Semlin camp outside Belgrade in Yugoslavia, a single van operated throughout the spring of 1942.[37] And in Minsk the commander of the Sipo-SD requested yet a fourth van in June 1942 to facilitate the "special handling" of weekly Jewish transports.[38] But this indicates the second reason for the rapid eclipse of the gas van. If it worked adequately only in the setting of a stationary camp, it was rendered obsolete almost immediately by the far more efficient gas chambers that were being put into operation in the first half of 1942.

Yet the history of the development and production of the gas van is instructive in several respects. First, it demonstrates the close connection between the euthanasia program in Germany, the *Einsatzgruppen* operations in Russia, and the death camps of Poland. Though not planned as such, the euthanasia program proved to be both a recruiting and a testing ground for the perpetrators of the Final Solution. Not only did the euthanasia institutes provide the gas chamber technology and personnel for the three camps of *Operation Reinhard* (Belzec, Sobibor, and Treblinka), but the euthanasia experience of the SS gassing experts of the KTI and *Sonderkommando* Lange provided the technology and personnel for the death camp at Chelmno. The impetus for developing the gas van came from problems encountered by the *Einsatzgruppen* in Russia. Artur Nebe, chief of both *Einsatzgruppe* B and the Kripo, had no trouble calling upon the resources of the RSHA to facilitate the *Einsatzgruppen* operations. But as plans for the Final Solution unfolded in the fall of 1941, the technology and personnel intended for Russia were available to be pressed into service on behalf of this even more ambitious program of mass murder aimed at all the European Jews. The logistical problems of building death camps and constructing networks of deportation meant that the major campaign could not get underway until the spring and summer of 1942. But in particular situations where local authorities urgently complained of lack of help from Berlin in solving the Jewish question, and the number of Jews to be murdered was not unmanageable, there was no need to wait. Berlin sent gas vans to Chelmno near Lodz and Semlin near Belgrade, and the local authorities were left to carry out the mass murders themselves. Thus the gas van, first utilized with bottled gas as part of the euthanasia program and then designed for the *Einsatzgruppen* operations by using exhaust gas, was pressed into service as a stopgap measure when the plans for the Final Solution in Europe were taking shape but the means were not yet available to carry it out.

Secondly, the gas-van episode illuminates the mentality of lower echelon figures entangled in the Final Solution. As Raul Hilberg has pointed out, the complex functions of modern society are carried out through a division of labor, and the Final Solution was no exception. In the Third Reich, specialists whose expertise normally had nothing to do with mass murder suddenly found themselves minor cogs in the machinery of destruction. As for the scientists, Becker was an *Altkämpfer* who had thrown in his political lot with the Nazis in 1930 and made his scientific expertise available to the local Gestapo as early as 1934, and Widmann was the "mad scientist" who became intoxicated with developing bizarre and novel instruments of death. Thus both, by their own initiative, had set themselves on a course of action that led not at all fortuitously to increasing complicity in mass murder. The same can scarcely be said for Pradel and his automotive experts, however. Occupied with procuring, dispatching, maintaining, and repairing motor vehicles, their expertise and facilities were suddenly pressed into the service of mass murder when they were charged with producing gas vans. In the course of half a year, some twenty vans passed through their shop, requiring only a moderate expenditure of time and energy on their part—a minor episode interrupting their normal routine. After the war they scarcely remembered, or not at all. The few who admitted they even knew that gas vans had been produced in their garage and for what purpose claimed to have been horrified and shocked. Their own documents portray a different picture. What disturbed them was the criticisms and complaints about the faults in their product. The shortcomings of the gas vans were a negative reflection on their worksmanship that had to be remedied! Kept fully abreast of the problems arising in the field, they strove for ingenious technical adjustments to make their product more efficient and acceptable to its operators. What could not be remedied had to be blamed on someone else; the explosion at Chelmno must have been due to operator error, they concluded. Their greatest concern seemed to be that they might be deemed inadequate to their assigned task.

Operating at a contact point between the initiated (the SS) and the uninitiated (Firma Gaubschat), these automotive experts developed the euphemistic code language so typical of the Final Solution—it hid reality from others and at least partially from themselves. Even in a memo intended solely for internal use, choking and dying Jews trying to escape became a "cargo" that shifted to the rear. Excrement, urine, vomit, and menstrual blood became "thicker filth" and "thin fluid" whose chief significance was not the agony it meant for the victims but the unloading, cleaning, and rusting problems that resulted for the perpetrators. Thus the automotive experts sought to cope simultaneously with both the production bottleneck and technical shortcomings of their product and the psychological burden of their task. They were more successful with the latter than with the former, though not for lack of trying.

4

The Semlin Gas Van
and the Final Solution
in Serbia

The extermination process in Serbia took place at the very beginning of the Final Solution in Europe and spanned the transition from firing squad to gassing. The first phase, as we have seen, consisted of mass shootings of Jews in the fall of 1941. Commencing just days before the first deportation of German Jewry in mid-October, these mass shootings were only partially analogous to the firing-squad operations of the *Einsatzgruppen* begun the previous summer in Russia. In Serbia the executioners were primarily German army personnel, not SS units, and the victims were males between the ages of fourteen and seventy, not entire families. Furthermore, the firing squads operated under the pretext of carrying out reprisals for casualties inflicted by the partisans, not with the avowed aim of exterminating the entire Jewish population. Uncertainty over the ultimate goal and scope of Nazi Jewish policy was not prolonged, however, as the murder of the Serbian Jews quickly moved into its second and final phase. The survivors of the fall massacres, mostly women and children, were placed in a concentration camp at Semlin just across the Sava River from Belgrade, and regardless of age or sex, were murdered in a gas van dispatched from the RSHA automotive department in Berlin. The last Jews of the Semlin camp had been gassed by early May 1942, before the Polish death camps of Treblinka and Sobibor were even in operation. If the Wehrmacht reprisal shootings of Serbian Jews in the fall of 1941 were still a prelude to the Final Solution, the gas-van murder of the Semlin Jews was one of the very first chapters of the Final Solution itself.

The Semlin *Judenlager*

After the Germans overran Yugoslavia in April 1941, the conquered country was immediately dismembered. Germany's allies received portions, and a *Ustashe* state was established in Croatia, while Serbia remained an occupation zone of the German army. In the frantic ten days between Yugoslavia's unexpected rejection of the pact with Germany and the invasion on April 6, hurried plans were made for this occupation. An order of the Army High Command (OKH) of April 2 provided for an *Einsatzgruppe* of the Sipo-SD to be responsible for the same tasks in Serbia that fell to these police organs in the Third Reich, especially combatting enemies of the state. This, of course, included Jews.[1] The *Einsatzgruppe* of SS-*Standartenführer* Dr. Wilhelm Fuchs was subordinate to the chief of the Military Administration, SS-*Gruppenführer* Dr. Harald Turner, who in turn reported directly to a rapid succession of military commanders— Schröder, Danckelmann, Böhme, and Bader—who paraded through Serbia in 1941. Thus, before the invasion, the Serbian Jews were consigned to the jurisdiction of the SS, but the military commander in Serbia retained overall command of and responsibility for occupation policy.

In the aftermath of the invasion, however, this simple delegation of Jewish affairs to the SS did not go unchallenged. In fact, a host of officials took part in effecting Germany's Jewish policy in Serbia. Within Turner's Military Administration were two officials in charge of political affairs concerning the Jews and Jewish property respectively. On the staff of the *Feldkommandantur* 599, the military district including Belgrade, of Colonel von Kaisenberg, were officials for Jewish affairs and Jewish apartments.[2] Presumably the other military districts likewise had their own Jewish experts, as a summary of Jewish affairs was a mandatory section of the required situation reports of the *Kreiskommandanturen* (subdistricts) to the *Feldkommandantur* 610.[3] Orders posted in Belgrade regulating Jewish shopping hours and curfew were issued over the name of the city commandant, Kaisenberg, while orders for various categories of Jews to register with the police were issued on the authority of the chief of the *Einsatzgruppe* of the Sipo-SD, Fuchs.[4] Overall jurisdiction of Jewish property was assigned to the Trusteeship Administration for Jewish Property within the office of the general plenipotentiary for the economy in Serbia, Franz Neuhausen, who reported to Göring, though the personal property and jewelry of the Jews was reluctantly conceded to the Sipo-SD.[5] And finally, the Foreign Office plenipotentiary, Felix Benzler, was charged to handle all questions emerging in Serbia that touched upon foreign affairs, which he and Ribbentrop understood to include freemasons and Jews.[6] In short, the chaotic administrative structure that typified the German occupation everywhere in Europe was fully evident in Serbia, Jewish policy included.

The Serbian Jews were quickly subjected to a wave of discriminatory measures: registration, marking, curfew, forced labor, restrictions on economic and social activities, and confiscation of property.[7] Their situation became graver in the summer of 1941 with the outbreak of the partisan uprising, as Jews increasingly and disproportionately fell victim to German reprisal and counterinsurgency terror measures. The Banat Jews were uprooted and taken to Belgrade in mid-August; subsequently all male Jews over fourteen in the Belgrade area, both local and from the Banat, were interned in the Topovske Šupe camp.[8] Beginning in early August the German Foreign Office plenipotentiary, Felix Benzler, allegedly acting on the suggestion of Harald Turner, urged repeatedly the deportation of the Serbian Jews (preferably to Rumania) as a necessary precondition for pacification of the country. Berlin rejected the deportation request, and subsequently the interned male Jews provided a convenient pool of victims for the German army's reprisal measures, now systematized on a one-hundred-to-one ratio. The "problem" of the male Jews solved, the Germans turned to the question of the women, children, and elderly, initially estimated at some twenty thousand. They were to be interned at a camp at Mitrovica, and deported to a "reception camp in the east" in the spring.[9]

The Mitrovica concentration camp, planned first at Jarak and then at Zasavica, proved unfeasible because both locations were too flooded for construction. On October 23, 1941, the decision was taken to abandon Mitrovica and use instead the exposition grounds—referred to as Semlin by the Germans and Sajmiste by the Yugoslavs—across the Sava River from Belgrade.[10] As that side of the Sava was Croatian territory, Benzler asked the German embassy in Zagreb to inquire if the exposition grounds could be used for a transit camp "in which at first Jewish women and children shall be brought." The Croatians agreed, provided the camp was guarded by Germans, not Serbs, and supplies came from Serbian, not Croatian, territory.[11] On the very day of the Croatian reply, Turner advised his regional commandants to prepare for the deportation of Jewish women and children to a collection camp near Belgrade sometime after November 15.[12]

Construction of the camp (conversion of the pavilions into huge barracks and the erection of barbed-wire fencing) was undertaken by *Organisation* Todt. It billed Turner's Military Administration for the cost of the material and labor; that in turn received funds to cover construction costs from the general plenipotentiary for the economy in Serbia.[13] It can be presumed that Neuhausen's outfit recovered this outlay from the accounts of its own Trusteeship Administration for Jewish property.[14] In less than one and one-half months after the military commander abandoned Mitrovica and selected the Semlin site, the camp was ready. On December 8, 1941, the surviving Jews in Belgrade were ordered to report to the police with several days' food supply and their lodging keys marked with name and address. They were immediately transferred to the Semlin camp.[15] While the "five kings of Serbia"—the military commander, Fuchs, Benzler, Turner, and Neuhausen—were notoriously unable to agree on most things, the selection, diplomatic negotiation, construction, and financing of the Semlin *Judenlager* proved a rare example of frictionless cooperation.

Life in the *Judenlager* was very harsh, especially in late December and January when the temperature dropped so low that the Sava River froze over. The huge exhibition halls were unheated. To maximize sleeping space so that thousands could be crammed into two large pavilions, multistoried wooden scaffolding had been constructed through which one had to crawl on hands and knees. In addition to hunger and cold, work details to shovel the nearby airfield took their toll. A prisoner "self-administration" was formed (the "camp elder" was a young woman under thirty named Sarfas), and met with the commandant each morning. Both the administrative and physical work in the camp was done by the Jews, even the patrolling of the inside of the fence to keep prisoners away from the wire. It was forbidden to bring food into the camp, and children who slipped through the unelectrified wire to beg in the suburb of Zemun were beaten if caught.[16]

In October the Germans had estimated the total number of Jewish women, children and elderly in Serbia at 20,000. In early December the military commander's staff expected 16,000 gypsies and Jews to be interned in Semlin.[17] Both estimates proved much too high. By December 15, 1941, the incarcerated Jews numbered 5,291.[18] As Jews from other parts of Serbia were deported to Semlin throughout the winter months, the total number of Jewish prisoners gradually rose. The two existing sets of figures do not agree, however: the Yugoslav records (of the Department of Social Welfare of the Belgrade municipal government) show a maximum of 6,800 prisoners by the end of February, and[19] German records report 5,780 at this time.[20] Another 500 Jews from Kosovska Mitrovica were deported to Semlin on March 19, which would have raised the total to 6,280.[21] According to the German commandant, Herbert Andorfer, at least 10 percent of the prisoners were gypsies.[22] It is possible the two different figures represent the total number of prisoners on the one hand and the Jewish prisoners on the other. In any case, neither reflects the considerable death rate over the winter months, and therefore the official Yugoslav estimate that 7,500 Jews died at Semlin seems quite reasonable.[23]

Even if the total number of prisoners in the Semlin *Judenlager* remained well below the Germans' initial expectations, provisioning of the camp was a problem. The initial arrangements provided that Turner would deposit money in an account of the Belgrade municipal government, which would deliver provisions to the camp. The camp commandant would verify the bills for the provisions received, to be checked against withdrawals from the account.[24] Almost immediately the Germans at the camp complained of inadequate supplies. On December 31, 1941, the first commandant, SS-*Scharführer* Edgar Enge, requested a doubling of the bread ration, which was immediately vetoed by *Oberkriegsverwaltungsrat* Dr. Ranze of the *Feldkommandantur* 599.[25] Nine days later Enge requested a 33 percent increase in the milk delivery because of the large number of sick children.[26] This was followed by a series of complaints about many unfilled orders and the poor quality of food delivered.[27] Finally, the new commandant, SS-*Untersturmführer* Herbert Andorfer, noting that the food ordered represented the absolute minimum required rations *(die tabellenmässig festgestellten Mindestmengen),* threatened that no bills would be verified until all orders were filled.[28] The Belgrade municipal government warned its Department of Social Welfare that the Germans were ready to prosecute those responsible for unfilled orders for urgently needed supplies.[29] Up to this point, at least, the German commandants were not behaving like men who knew they were soon going to murder their prisoners.

Thereafter, however, the complaints ran in the other direction. The initial German payment to the Belgrade municipal government was exhausted in February, and the latter loaned money to the account while requesting payment from the Germans that was finally forthcoming in mid-March.[30] In April Mayor Dragomir-Dragi Jovanovic requested another payment, which was not forthcoming until mid-June. The Germans still owed a small balance, but the thrifty Dr. Ranze noted that many bills submitted by the Serbs seemed too high and recommended that a commission be formed to check them. Well aware that the *Judenlager* no longer existed, Ranze recommended that any items delivered to the camp that were not significantly depreciated be turned over to the Quartermaster's Office of the *Feldkommandantur* for use elsewhere.[31]

The German Security Police in Belgrade

Shortly after the Semlin camp opened in December 1941, a major reorganization of the German police in Serbia occurred. Hitherto the *Einsatzgruppe* of the Sipo-SD under Fuchs reported to Turner, an SS-*Gruppenführer* but a man whose office was directly subordinate to the military commander. Himmler now recalled Fuchs and disbanded the *Einsatzgruppe.* In its place he installed a Higher SS and Police Leader, August Meyszner, an SS-*Gruppenführer* like Turner and thus not outranked. Meyszner's instructions in questions relating to military affairs came from the military commander, not from Turner. His instructions concerning police matters came directly from Berlin.[32] Under Meyszner's overall coordination were both the Security Police and Security Service (Sipo-SD) and the Order Police *(Ordnungspolizei),* though each received specific instructions from its main office in Berlin as well. The new head of the Sipo-SD, who would be directly in charge of the Semlin camp and its Jewish prisoners, was SS-*Standartenführer* Emanuel Schäfer.

Born in 1900 the son of a hotel proprietor, Schäfer was reared in the German border area of Upper Silesia.[33] Upon completion of his gymnasium studies he was drafted into the army in the summer of 1918, joined an artillery regiment in Berlin, but did not see front service. He returned home and immediately took up with various German paramilitary formations battling Poles in Upper Silesia. His home town, Rybnik, went to

Poland in the partition, but he renounced Polish citizenship and took up university studies at Breslau, attaining his doctorate in jurisprudence in 1925. He joined the *Stahlhelm,* the nationalistic veterans' organization, in the same year and began a career in the police, first in Potsdam and then in Breslau, where he headed the homocide division from 1928 to 1933. He left the *Stahlhelm* in 1928 because he had "the impression that the *Stahlhelm* was atrophying" *(den Eindruck, dass der Stahlhelm im Absterben begriffen war).*[34] Three years later, impressed by the Nazis' "vitality" but contemptuous of "party book officials," Schäfer became a "supporting member" *(förderndes Mitglied)* of the SS but not a party member of the NSDAP.

Within weeks of the Nazi assumption of power Schäfer was made head of the political police in Breslau. He applied to the NSDAP in May 1933, only to find out more than a year later that his application had been rejected, presumably because of a grudge in connection with the sodomy proceedings he had lodged against the erstwhile *Gauleiter* Helmut Brückner. Schäfer's position was made even more difficult when SA-*Obergruppenführer* Edmund Heines, one of the most notorious members of Ernst Röhm's homosexual clique of SA-leaders, took over the Breslau police and had Schäfer enrolled in the SA. "More drawn" to the SS, Schäfer became an agent for its intelligence network, the SD, reporting on corruption of various party officials, especially Heines, who was subsequently shot in the Blood Purge of June 30, 1934. A promotion recommendation in Schäfer's file noted his performance: "After the seizure of power, as head of the State Police in Breslau, which was subordinate to Edmund Heines at that time, he [Schäfer] cooperated with the SD-RFSS and rendered valuable service despite great danger to himself."[35] *(Nach der Machtübernahme hat er als Leiter der Staatspolizei in Breslau, die damals Edmund Heines unterstellt war, trotz grosser Gefahr für sich mit dem* SD-RFSS *zusammengearbeitet und diesem wertvolle Dienste geleistet.)*

In May 1934 Schäfer was named chief of the State Police Agency (Staatspolizeistelle) in Oppeln, where he continued his SD work as well. His belated transfer from the SA to the SS in September 1936 was quickly compensated with three promotions in twenty-six months. Heydrich's implicit trust in his longtime SD agent was demonstrated in the summer of 1939. On August 10 Schäfer received a telephone call to meet Heydrich at the airport. Heydrich informed him that the Führer "needs a pretext for war" *(braucht einen Kriegsgrund)* and had Schäfer guide him to several border points as possible locations to stage border attacks on German territory. A week later both Himmler and Heydrich visited, and this time, again guided by Schäfer, surveyed the border from the air. A customs house was decided upon, and on the night of August 31, following an earlier last-minute postponement, a fake attack upon the customs house was staged (independent of the Gleiwitz incident).[36] In the same month

Schäfer was named head of *Einsatzgruppe* II for the Polish campaign, which distinguished itself by the comparatively high number of executions it reported.[37]

At the end of the Polish campaign, the *Einsatzgruppen* were dissolved and Schäfer was made chief of the *Staatspolizeistelle* in Kattowitz, from which two thousand Jews were deported to Eichmann's Nisko camp in late October.[38] Schäfer was transferred to the *Staatspolizeistelle* in Köln in October 1940 and oversaw the first three deportations of Jews from that city the following year—two thousand to Lodz on October 21 and 28 and another one thousand to Riga on December 6, 1941.[39] In January 1942 Schäfer was summoned to Berlin to meet with Heydrich, who appointed him commander of the Sipo-SD in Belgrade, allegedly because his earlier experiences in the post–World War I Polish border struggles made him especially suited for antipartisan fighting. According to Schäfer, Heydrich said nothing about the Jewish question in Serbia at this meeting.[40]

Belgrade's new police chief was a valuable Heydrich recruit—a borderland German ultranationalist and convinced National Socialist of proven loyalty to the SS, but at the same time a well-educated, well-trained, highly experienced police technocrat. Other German officials with whom he came into contact were pleasantly surprised to discover that Schäfer, unlike his predecessor Fuchs or his supervisor Meyszner, was not a "pigheaded SS man" *(ein sturer SS-Mann)*. On the contrary, he made a "thoroughly humane impression" *(einen durchaus menschlichen Eindruck)*. He was "reasonable" and "very accommodating."[41] Postwar judicial authorities were equally impressed by his bearing; he was a "correct and honest official *(korrekt und sauberer Beamter)* who was "not to be viewed as an evil Gestapo-functionary, rather as an official who—to be sure an enthusiastic National Socialist with early knowledge of the criminal practices—did his duty, but showed humane tendencies and endeavoured to remedy the excesses of the regime"[42] *(nicht als ein Gestapo-funktionär üblen Gepräges anzusehen, vielmehr als ein Beamter zu betrachten ist, der—zwar begeisterter Nationalsozialist mit frühzeitiger Kenntnis von den verbrecherischen Pratiken—seine Pflict getan, aber menschliche Züge gezeigt hat und bemüht gewesen ist, Auswüchsen des Regimes abzuhelfen)*. "Beloved" by his close circle of secretary, driver, and adjutant,[43] Schäfer presented quite a different face to the slack and frequently corrupt personnel he inherited from Fuchs. To them he was an arrogant, strict, unapproachable superior who imposed "iron discipline" and before whom they made exaggerated bows when he appeared. It was said among Schäfer's men, "For him mankind begins only at the rank of captain"[44] *(Der Mensch finge bei ihm erst mit dem Hauptsturmführer an)*.

To Heydrich, Schäfer's veneer of respectability was no doubt useful but more important was his unblemished record as an utterly reliable agent—successful SD spy against SA rivals, trusted conspirator on the eve of war, ruthless *Einsatzgruppen* commander in Poland, and deporter of Jews from Kattowitz and Köln. That Serbia would be only the second territory of the German empire declared *judenfrei* shortly after Schäfer's arrival was scarcely out of keeping with his past record.

Upon assuming his position in Belgrade, Schäfer took over Fuchs's personnel but reorganized the dissolved *Einsatzgruppe* into divisions paralleling the RSHA structure in Berlin, ending what he claimed to be the petty rivalry and bickering between Sipo, SD, and Kripo.[45] Division IV was the Gestapo under *Sturmbannführer* Bruno Sattler. Born in 1898 the son of a civil engineer, Sattler had served two years at the front in World War I. His postwar involvement in the Potsdam *Freikorps* culminated in the Kapp Putsch. Settling down to school Sattler completed six semesters of university study, when the inflation wiped out his family's property. He had to seek work and eventually entered the criminal police in 1928. He joined the NSDAP in 1931 and the SS in 1936. He served in the Gestapo in Paris before coming to Belgrade.[46]

Within the Gestapo was the Jewish Desk or *Judenreferat,* staffed by four Germans and four *Volksdeutschen* from the Banat.[47] Two of the Germans served as commandant of the Semlin *Judenlager* and would take part in the gas-van operation: *Untersturmführer* Herbert Andorfer and *Scharführer* Edgar Enge. Born out of wedlock in 1911, Andorfer was reared and supported by his mother in Salzburg, Austria. He completed his *Matura* in 1929, with grades adequate for university entrance, but family finances did not permit further study other than vocational training for hotel work. He worked two summers as a hotel secretary in Bad Ischl but was otherwise unemployed, except for a stint as a door-to-door salesman, until he became secretary and eventually business manager of a hotel in Sölden am Ötztal from 1934 to 1938. During his period of unemployment Andorfer joined the NSDAP in October 1931 and the SS in September 1933. He maintained his SS membership during the "illegal" period and smuggled party literature from Germany. Andorfer became *Ortsgruppenleiter* in Sölden immediately following the Anschluss, but in May 1938 left for Innsbruck to make his career in the SS rather than the hotel business. His application for the Waffen-SS was rejected, but Andorfer was sent to the university in Innsbruck while he worked for the SD on public opinion and blackmarket activities. His university days ended with the outbreak of war, and following a warning for violating party discipline because of derogatory comments about his superiors, Andorfer was transferred first to Salzburg and then to the Sipo-SD training camp in Pretzsch. He took part in the invasion of Yugoslavia, served in various SD outposts, and then joined the Belgrade staff, where he was made commandant of the Semlin *Judenlager* at the end of January 1942.[48]

The man whom Andorfer succeeded as camp commandant was Edgar Enge.[49] Enge was born in 1905 in Thuringia but his family soon moved to Leipzig. His father had failed at poultry farming, but until the mid-1920s supported the family as a salesman. Enge apprenticed for an office equipment firm in 1923 for two years and found steady work from 1926 to 1930. Then both he and his father were unemployed; in the family only Enge's brother had a steady job. It was not until 1935 that Enge found steady work again, as a tourist guide for the city of Leipzig. In the meantime he had joined the SA in 1933 because "it was expected of all young men to be politically active in some way" *(es wurde von allen jüngeren Menschen erwartet, dass sie sich irgendwie politisch betätigten)* and he hoped it would help him find work. He joined the party only in 1938 and was drafted in 1940. Instead of being taken into the army, however, the thirty-five-year-old Enge was sent to a *Schutzpolizei* training camp. After two months' training, and by no initiative of his own, he claimed, Enge was selected by the Sipo and sent for a probationary training period to the Frankfurt Gestapo. He successfully requested transfer to Leipzig, only to be sent to Yugoslavia in the summer of 1941. An employee of the Gestapo but not a member of the SS, he received the SS uniform and rank of *Scharführer* commensurate with his Gestapo rank.[50] At what point Enge was assigned to the *Judenreferat* is unclear, but he was present at at least one massacre of Jews in the fall of 1941, and confessed to being present at a number of reprisal shootings.[51] He served as commandant of the Semlin *Judenlager* in December and January, until the higher-ranking Andorfer took over.

The two SS-officers in charge of the Jews in Semlin, Schäfer and Sattler, were thus from upper-middle-class backgrounds and had already involved themselves in postwar paramilitary activities even before personal misfortune struck (Schäfer's home town was allotted to Poland and Sattler's family fortune was wiped out in the inflation). Both pursued a university education and a career in the police before committing themselves to the Nazis in 1931. The two SS-men who would be faced with carrying out the murders in person, Andorfer and Enge, were of lower-middle-class background and vocation, and had thrown in their lot with the Nazis while experiencing prolonged unemployment and economic distress. The murder of the Serbian Jews would be carried out by a typical SS-division of labor between well-trained and well-educated organizers and the executioners mobilized from Germany's depressed lower middle class.

The Gas Van at Semlin

The circumstances surrounding the actual decision to send a gas van to Belgrade are unclear, due to conflicting accounts. On April 11, 1942, Harald Turner wrote to Karl Wolff, Himmler's adjutant:

> Already some months ago I had all the available Jews shot and all Jewish women and children concentrated in a camp and at the same time, with the help of the SD, procured a 'delousing truck' that will finally clear the camp in some 14 days to 4 weeks, which in any case since the arrival of Meyssner [sic] and the transfer of this camp business to him, has been carried on by him.[52]

(Schon vor Monaten habe ich alles an Juden im hiesigen Lande greifbare erschiessen und sämtliche Judenfrauen und Kinder in einem Lager konzentrieren lassen und zugleich mit Hilfe des SD einer 'Entlausungswagen' angeschaft, der nun in etwa 14 Tage bis 4 Wochen auch die Räumung des Lagers endgültig durchgeführt haben wird, was allerdings seit Eintreffen von Meyssner und Übergabe dieser Lagerdinge an ihn, von ihm weitergeführt worden ist.)

Turner's claim in April 1942 to have initiated the sending of the gas van is suspect on two counts. First, the preceding reports of Turner that have survived in SS files indicate no such initiative. Turner was quite content to boast of his clearing Belgrade of Jews and their placement in a concentration camp.[53] Secondly, Turner's reports to Berlin were often inaccurate and very self-serving. He was fighting desperately to protect himself from the threats to his position posed both by the military, which was trying to downgrade the position of the chief of the Military Administration, and from Himmler, who was establishing a Higher SS and Police Leader with jurisdiction over many areas formerly allotted to Turner, especially the police. Thus Turner made many exaggerated and in some cases totally false claims about his role in Jewish affairs, among others, in a desperate but unsuccessful attempt to impress Himmler.[54]

If it was self-serving of Turner during the war to exaggerage his role in the murder of the Serbian Jews, it was equally self-serving of Schäfer after the war to downgrade his role. Schäfer emphatically insisted that he had not discussed the Jewish question in Serbia with Heydrich prior to his departure for Belgrade, and that neither his nor any other agency in Serbia had instigated the sending of the gas van. On the other hand, he admitted to having heard of the gas van's being used to kill the mentally ill very shortly after the outbreak of the war (a *Sonderkommando* led by Herbert Lange was headquartered in Posen and used gas vans to carry out euthanasia operations in the incorporated territories while Schäfer was in Kattowitz). He claimed not to have known yet of the *Einsatzgruppen* operations in Russia (since this admission would have made him accessory to murder for the deportation of Köln Jews to Riga). Schäfer did admit that, upon hearing shortly after his arrival in Belgrade of the massacre of the male Jews the previous fall, he was convinced the destruction of the European Jews had been decided in Berlin. Thus, he knew immediately what was intended when a telegram arrived from SS-*Obergruppenführer* Heinrich Müller, the chief of the Gestapo in Berlin, reading (as best Schäfer could recall):

Subject: Jewish operation in Serbia. Commando with special Saurer truck underway overland with special assignment.

(Betrifft: Judenaktion in Serbien. Einsatzkommando mit Spezialwagen Saurer auf dem Landwege mit Spezialauftrage unterwegs.)

Unusual in his refusal to spread responsibility as widely as possible, Schäfer was explicit that the telegram came directly from Berlin to him, and that neither Meyszner, the military, nor any other German agency in Serbia was involved, though Meyszner was kept informed.[55]

If the contradictory accounts of Turner and Schäfer cannot be relied upon fully, some facts are not in dispute. The Foreign Office plenipotentiary, Felix Benzler, had urged the deportation of all Jews the previous August. When the male Jews were shot, it was agreed in a late October meeting attended by one of Eichmann's representatives from Berlin, Friedrich Suhr, that the women and children would be interned and deported to a "reception camp in the east" as soon as this was technically possible. In December Benzler reiterated his plea that the Jews be deported as soon as possible, and the prospect of the following spring at the earliest was held out.[56] After Schäfer's arrival, Benzler urged upon him the deportation of the Semlin Jews to Rumania as well. For both Schäfer and Benzler the Jewish camp with its complicated procedures—located on Croatian territory, provisioned by the Serbs, guarded by the *Ordnungspolizei* on the outside and administered by the Sipo on the inside—was "extraordinarily burdensome" *(ausserordentlich lästig)*.[57] None of the German occupation authorities were anxious to see the existence of the *Judenlager* prolonged. At the Wannsee Conference on January 20, 1942, Heydrich announced his intention to carry out deportations from west to east. This meant that Serbia would not be relieved of its Jews through deportation in the near future, and Heydrich could anticipate further complaint over this new delay. At the same time gas vans, produced for the explicit purpose of gassing Jewish women and children whose execution by shooting was proving too burdensome, were being completed in Heydrich's Sipo garage.

Given these facts it seems not wildly hypothetical to speculate that the decision practically made itself: local authorities in Belgrade wanted to get rid of their relatively small number of Jewish women and children, whom unlike the men the army would not shoot, and had been led to believe this would occur in the spring. Heydrich, however, was not planning deportations in the area for the coming year, but he happened to have the gas vans that were designed to kill precisely these categories of Jews. If Belgrade wanted to be rid of its Jews, Heydrich would provide them with the equipment to do the job themselves.

Such an interpretation is consistent with events elsewhere at this time, when the Germans had decided to kill the European Jews but did not yet have the means to do it. When the authorities in Lodz complained about additional shipments of German Jews to their overcrowded ghetto, suddenly Lange's *Sonderkommando* of gas vans was transferred from Posen to Chelmno and began reducing the Lodz ghetto. When Hans Frank, who had long pressed for the Jews of the General Government to be shipped elsewhere, sent his state secretary, Bühler, to Berlin in December 1941, he learned that Berlin was no longer planning to deport Polish Jews. Frank and his men would have to kill the Jews themselves, though Berlin would show them how.[58] Belgrade too had pestered Berlin to deport its Jews; now Berlin sent a gas van instead.

Martin Broszat has suggested that the Final Solution emerged from a series of uncoordinated and spontaneous local murder actions. From above, the Nazi leadership constantly pressed for a solution to the Jewish question in the form of deportation to Russia. However, the military campaign stalled, deportations backed up, and local authorities took the initiative to relieve the pressure through murdering some of their own Jews. As the massacres became more widespread and systematic, the conception of the Final Solution emerged after the fact, and not from some comprehensive order from above.[59] My interpretation, if correct, would indicate a chain of causation in the opposite direction. The Nazi leadership had decided upon the physical extermination of the Jews but did not immediately possess the means to accomplish this. However, Berlin did not always have to sit idly by when local authorities complained about lack of help in dealing with their Jews. When feasible, those who complained could be sent gas vans to do the "dirty work" themselves. In short, it was not pressure from above for deportation that caused local leaders to kill; rather, it was pressure from below for deportation that caused the central authorities to provide the means to kill locally, at least until the death camps were ready.

Upon receiving the telegram from Müller, Schäfer informed Sattler of its contents, instructed him to do what was necessary, and awaited the arrival of the van. When the two drivers, SS-*Scharführer* Götz and Meyer, were taken to Schäfer, they explained to him their assignment to kill the Jews in the Semlin camp, which came as no surprise. Schäfer sent them to Sattler, in whose hands allegedly he thereafter left the entire operation. He did, however, bestir himself sufficiently to witness the gas van operation once.[60]

In early March the *Judenlager* commandant, Herbert Andorfer, was summoned, whether by Schäfer or Sattler (to whom he reported once every eight or ten days) he was later not sure. The Jews, he was told, were about to be "resettled" in a "special truck" from Germany in which they would be "put to sleep." *(eingeschläfert)* Andorfer was to accompany the gas van to assure secrecy of the operation. To avoid any search of the van when it crossed the Sava River from Croatian to Serbian territory, he was provided with special papers. A detachment of police would guard against intruders during the unloading and burial.[61]

Andorfer was upset at the prospect of returning to face those who were soon to die. As camp commandant he had worked for more than a month with the camp's "self-administration" and become personally acquainted with about fifty of the prisoners. By his own account he had even drunk coffee and played cards with some of the prisoners in the camp administration after they had learned not to fear him. He had previously dodged answering questions on the whereabouts of their husbands, and concerning their future, had routinely said that eventually they were all to be sent to Rumania. Now, when he told them that first they would be resettled in another transit camp in Yugoslavia, they pressed him for details about the new camp. Andorfer typed up a fictitious set of camp regulations to end this questioning that he now found so disconcerting.

When the *Aktion* began, the gas van parked outside the camp entrance for loading, while a second, open truck entered the camp to pick up the baggage of those being resettled. One of the drivers of the gas van strolled about the camp, collected the children around him, and passed out candy.[62] A Jewish doctor or nurse was selected to accompany each transport. The deception was complete, and initially there was no shortage of volunteers. It was arranged among the prisoners that messages were to be written on the baggage truck, giving news of the new camp, but no messages were ever found in the predetermined locations. Eventually, the supply of volunteers dried up, lists were then compiled by the Germans, and the deportees were summoned day by day. Even then the Jewish prisoners had no inkling of their imminent fate.[63]

Once loaded, the truck drove to the Sava bridge just several hundred meters from the camp entrance, where Andorfer waited in a car so as not to have to witness the loading. The bridge had been damaged and only one span was drivable; thus traffic alternated directions. The departure was timed, however, so that the gas van would never have to wait for oncoming traffic before crossing. The police license plates ensured that no attempt was made to control the truck, and Andorfer never needed to show the special papers. On the far side of the bridge, the gas van stopped and one of the drivers climbed out and worked underneath it, connecting the exhaust to the sealed compartment. The baggage truck turned off the road, while the gas van and the commandant's car drove through the middle of Belgrade to reach a shooting range at Avala (Avelar in the German documents) ten kilometers to the southeast of the city.

At the Avala shooting range a grave had already been dug and a guard detachment from the 64th Reserve Police Battalion of the *Ordnungspolizei* was waiting. The 64th Reserve Police Battalion (later renamed the 1st Batallion of the 5th SS-Police Regiment) had been involved in antipartisan activities and reprisal shootings since the previous summer. It had also had more mundane watch duties; for instance, teams of twenty-five policemen alternated as guards outside the Semlin camp. In early March Karl W., a veteran of the *Schutzpolizei* since 1935 and stationed in Yugoslavia since the previous summer, was summoned to report with three other men to the Sipo headquarters in Belgrade. He chose his friend, Paul S., and then asked the two men who happened to be in the next room, Leo L. and Karl L.[64] At police headquarters they were warned of the top secrecy of their coming assignment and told to report to the Belgrade jail the following morning.

Upon reporting for duty they were instructed to guard a detachment of seven Serbian prisoners. A police truck, driven by a man in an SD uniform, took them all to the Avala shooting range, where they met up with the vehicles from Semlin. As a large moving-van type truck backed up to the grave, Andorfer explained to Karl W. that it was a gas van carrying Jews from the Semlin camp. W. was to position his men to guard both the entrance and the prisoners, who were to unload the corpses from the van into the grave. When the doors were opened, many of the bodies pressing against them fell out. The Serbian prisoners completed their gruesome task in under an hour, and W. was told to return again the next morning.

Andorfer had already approached his fellow Austrian, Hans Rexeisen, head of Division III of the Belgrade Sipo-SD, about a transfer to other duties. Rexeisen had told him he would get him assigned to an anti-Chetnik unit, but nothing came of it. Now, after witnessing the first unloading of the gas van, Andorfer made a written request to Schäfer for military duty with the Waffen-SS. His job, he said, could be handled by someone not fit for combat duty. No transfer was forthcoming, but Edgar Enge, his predecessor as commandant at Semlin, was now assigned to share the job. At first they drove together, but later alternated. Enge made no attempt to be transferred. Because the work was so unattractive, he was only surprised that the participants in the operation received no present or reward for their services.[65] The four policemen talked among themselves and concluded they had been badly used. But they feared to approach their superior with a request for transfer, because they had been sworn to secrecy and the request might be reported to the SD. They too, therefore, carried on.[66]

Thus the same people—Andorfer and Enge, the gas-van drivers Götz and Meyer, the four policemen and the seven Serbian prisoners—repeated the horrifying procedure over and over again for two months. Every morning, except Sundays and holidays, and usually two or three afternoons a week as well, the gas van traveled from Semlin to Avala. The large Saurer van, able to carry fifty male adults, was often filled with one hundred women and children for each trip.[67] On May 10, 1942, the van, accompanied by Enge, made its last deadly trip, taking the Jewish camp administration. After the final unloading, the Serbian prisoners, who had earlier been told that they would be sent to work in Norway, were shot.[68] Because of a damaged rear axle, the gas van and its drivers returned to Berlin by train.[69] The four policemen got their annual three weeks' leave, and an extra week of special leave, which one of them told a friend was "squarely deserved" *(redlich verdient)*, and a private train compartment courtesy of the Sipo-SD for the ride back to Germany.[70] The *Judenreferat* having become superfluous, Andorfer was now granted his request for antipartisan combat duty and transferred to the Sipo-SD outpost in Novi Pazar. Schäfer, Sattler, and Enge remained in Belgrade, and the Semlin camp was filled immediately with other prisoners.

The Semlin camp had not been selected for the inaccessibility or secrecy of its location. One side of it lay alongside the highway that ran between the Sava River bridge and the suburb of Zemun, where the airport, German radio station, and headquarters of Neuhausen's agency were located. It was a highway well traveled by the German occupiers. Along another side of the camp ran the Sava River itself, across from which rose the heights of Belgrade. From the higher parts of the city anyone could look across the river and down into the camp. In 1941 this did not bother the Germans, who had come to the Balkans as the new *Herrenvolk* confident of victory and relatively unconcerned about the public display of their atrocities. It was only in late 1943, when the tide of war had clearly changed and a belated attempt was being made to put a more "humane" face on German occupation policies, that anyone seemed concerned. The new German ambassador, Hermann Neubacher, requested that the Semlin camp be moved because its continuing existence "before the eyes of the people of Belgrade was politically intolerable for reasons for public feelings"[71] *(von der Augen der Belgrader Bevölkerung aus stimmungsmässen Gründen für politisch nicht tragbar).* Neubacher's request was ignored, and ultimately some forty-seven thousand people perished there.[72]

The perpetrators of the Final Solution in Serbia wasted no time in making their achievement known to higher authorities in both Berlin and the Balkans. In an overview of measures against Jews in occupied territories, the Foreign Office Jewish expert noted on May 29, 1942, that "The Jewish question in Serbia is no longer acute. Now it is only a matter there of settling the legal questions concerning property."[73] *(Die Judenfrage ist in Serbien nicht mehr akut. Es handelt sich dort nur noch um die Regelung vermögensrechtlicher Fragen.)* Ten days later, on June 8, 1942, Schäfer informed a gathering of Wehrmacht officers, including the commanding general in Serbia, Paul Bader, and Military Commander Southeast, Walter Kuntze, who was visiting from his headquarters in Greece, that there was no longer a Jewish question in Serbia.[74]

The gassing of the Jews of the Semlin *Judenlager* was also no secret among the Germans on the spot. In Schäfer's agency it was of course immediately known—an "open secret."[75] The van, after all, was parked in the courtyard of the police headquarters and cleaned out by its drivers there after every operation.[76] As both this courtyard and the Semlin camp, in addition to the burial site, were guarded by men from the 64th Reserve Police Battalion, word soon circulated among them as well.[77] Schäfer himself conceded that it was impossible to prevent talk about the gas van, though he himself was one of the greatest offenders of confidentiality, not only to his own staff but to an army medical doctor to whom he remarked "with pride" that "Belgrade was the only great city of Europe that was free of Jews."[78] The judicial expert on Turner's staff was asked in the spring of 1942 by his *Volksdeutsche* cleaning woman if he knew "that the Jewish women were being destroyed in a gas van."[79] A German soldier with friends in the Sipo-SD who had already heard much of the firing squad executions of Jews and Serbs the previous fall—details of the executions were the frequent topic of mealtime conversation—now also learned of the gas van.[80] Indeed, even German soldiers without SS connections learned of it.[81] Rumors of the gas van spread among the nearby Croatian Jews, who had not yet been interned, and even as far as the Serbian Jewish refugees who had escaped to Hungary.[82] Clearly, if the Germans could drive a gas van through downtown Belgrade day after day while its passengers screamed and pounded against the back door in their death agony, secrecy was not the highest priority at the time, except in regard to the unsuspecting victims still in camp. Later, however, traces of the mass murder had to be erased. In December, 1943, Paul Blobel's *Kommando* 1005, charged with digging up and burning the bodies from the mass graves left behind by the *Einsatzgruppen* in Russia, arrived in Yugoslavia, and liquidated the mass graves near Avala, among others.[83]

In terms of numbers of victims, the murder of some seventy-five hundred Jews in Semlin was a minor episode in the Holocaust. Yet, in terms of personnel and timing, it is instructive. Many of the personnel of the death camps in Poland came either from the Death's Head units, with experience in the German concentration camp system, or from the euthanasia program. Even if one disregards the supporting cast of diplomats, bureaucrats, and military officers involved in German Jewish policy in Serbia and concentrates solely on the SS, the personnel involved in the Semlin gassings were not veterans hardened by their experience in euthanasia or the concentration camp system. Yugoslavia was a marginal theater compared with the momentous military operations and occupation policies underway in the east. Just as Yugoslavia received second-rate military units for the most part, so the SS personnel, with the exception of Schäfer, were men with relatively nondescript and unspectacular SS careers. In Semlin, however, the lack of special training or experience did not prove to be a barrier to mass murder.

Much has been written of the SS as an ideologically indoctrinated, highly disciplined, loyal, and obedient elite, primed to carry out Hitler's most radical policies. While these aspects are important, they have perhaps overshadowed other essential factors. The SS was a multifaceted organization, a reservoir of manpower that disposed of many skills and specialties. Specialization and division of labor, keys to man's productivity, were also keys to the SS's capacity to wreak destruction. Organizers and technicians were as important as executioners; the breadth of skills as important as discipline and ideological commitment.

Division of labor and specialization were not only important for the potential efficiency placed in the hands of the organizers of mass murder. They also routinized and compartmentalized the participation of the lower-echelon perpetrators, greatly enhancing their capacity to continue acting on a "business-as-usual" basis. The members of the *Einsatzgruppen* confronted the murderous reality of their actions every day, and both the inefficiency and psychological burden of the killing method were soon apparent to the organizers. In contrast, the development of the gas van and its use to murder the Semlin Jews presaged the efficiency and routinized detachment of the death camps. Guards continued to guard, whether it was a bridge, a concentration camp, or a mass-burial site. Drivers drove, whether it was a chauffeured limousine or a gas van. Chemists worked in their crime lab, whether to solve murders or facilitate them. Mechanics worked in their garages on all vehicles, whatever their function, and motor-pool supervisors procured and dispatched them. Camp commandants kept order in their camps, whether it required threatening Serbs to deliver the minimal food supplies to keep their prisoners alive one month or inventing fictitious regulations of a bogus transit camp to send the same prisoners unsuspecting to their deaths the next one.

For Andorfer, who had come to know some of the Semlin Jews as individual human beings, the mass murder admittedly caused distress. But compartmentalization of functions provided solace. He was responsible for keeping order among the living in the camp, and for keeping secrecy over the dead. The intervening killing operation was not his job. He waited by the bridge for the van in the morning; after lunch, he visited the camp in the afternoon. He was no murderer, he claimed. He did not design the gas van or send it from Berlin, he did not load the prisoners, he did not connect the pipe or drive the truck. "The murderer was my government! . . . It was a desk murder" in which the organizers made use of "the little people." *(Der Mörder war meine Regierung! . . . Das war ein Schreibtischmord!)*[84]

For a few in higher positions, like Schäfer, the murder of the Semlin Jews was a chance to win further recognition in their highly successful careers. A terse telegram announcing the arrival of a special truck conveyed without specifics all that was expected by Schäfer's superiors, and he did not disappoint them. For most, however, excepting the driver who chose to gather the Jewish children around him and pass out candy, the direct and intimate realization of their participation in mass murder was avoidable. The victims could remain a dehumanized abstraction, their own actions just a small incident in a long career. It was not initiative and resourcefulness, merely the psychological detachment to continue their usual jobs in unusual circumstances that made the mass murder possible.

The trail of complicity is long—from the mechanic, motor-pool boss, chemists, and chief of technical affairs in Berlin to the guards, drivers, camp commandants, and police chief in Belgrade. All were part of the

SS's police network, and more had a police-career background prior to being absorbed into the SS than an SS background that gained them entry into the police. Clearly no quantitative judgments can be drawn from a limited case study, but it does suggest that the institutional features and personnel of the German police deserve as much attention as the ideology and discipline of the SS.

The question of timing in Serbia is also important. The period from the spring of 1941, with the formation of the *Einsatzgruppen,* to the spring of 1942, with the opening of the death camp at Belzec in mid-March, is a confused time span in the history of German Jewish policy. As we have seen, the decision-making process at the highest level of Nazi leadership is not clearly revealed in documentation. Thus a wide variety of interpretations has flourished. Because of this lack of definitive documentation at the highest level, the attempt must be made to reconstruct the decision-making process through its reflection at lower levels.

A study of the Serbian case alone will not resolve this controversy. However, it does indicate that a fundamental shift took place in German Jewish policy in Serbia between the fall of 1941 and the spring of 1942. The killing of the male Jews emerged primarily out of local factors related to the partisan war and the army's reprisal policy. The male Jews were a convenient and expendable pool of victims, whose executions would satisfy the required reprisal quotas without producing undesired political repercussions aggravating the antipartisan struggle. Berlin sent SS and Foreign Office representatives to Belgrade to urge a "local solution" to the Jewish question. They discovered upon arrival that their pressure was unnecessary, for a local solution was already underway. The fall murders were not a conscious part of a European-wide Final Solution to the Jewish question, but it would appear that such a plan was already conceived, if not yet ready to be implemented, at this time. The Belgrade authorities and Berlin representatives agreed that the Jewish women, children, and elderly would be placed in a concentration camp and sent to a "reception camp in the east" (clearly no labor camp was meant for these categories of Jews!) as soon as this was technically feasible. No such "reception camp" as yet existed nor, it turned out, was deportation to one possible as soon as Belgrade wished. Another solution proved more feasible—to send a gas van to Belgrade. This was not a spontaneous local massacre, merely encouraged and abetted by Berlin, but the consummation in Serbia of a wider plan to destroy the European Jews. The pride with which Schäfer boasted of his accomplishments—"Belgrade was the only great city of Europe that was free of Jews," and his Sipo-SD *Dienststelle* only the second outside Germany to report its territory *judenfrei*[85]—and the zeal with which Turner sought to gain a share of the credit indicates that both were fully aware of how these events were perceived in Berlin.

Conclusion

How does a mass-murder program like the Final Solution begin? That is a question without a simple answer, for the emergence of the Final Solution was a mosaic of many pieces. It did not result from a single decision by Hitler to implement his long-held plans, nor was it carried out by a monolithic power structure simply responding through blind obedience to explicit instructions from above. By the summer of 1941, with the political repression of their internal enemies, the bloody occupation policies in Poland, euthanasia, and the inauguration of the *Vernichtungskrieg* and *Einsatzgruppen* massacres in Russia behind them, the Nazis had long crossed the "moral rubicon" of mass murder. What was new to the Nazis was the fantastic victories over Russia that held out the imminent and intoxicating prospect of an entire continent at their feet and the chance to make history according to their dictates.

No matter for how long or how concretely Hitler may have fantasized the mass murder of the Jews, however, one man and one decision could not do it alone. Hitler could give the "green light" but it required the initiative and zeal of others to make the Final Solution a reality. In an atmosphere pervaded by anti-Semitism[1]—one in which most Germans readily identified the Jews as enemies—and acclimatized to mass murder as a widely practiced state policy, the problem was not how to find killers but how to devise a method of mass murder capable of dealing with the anticipated numbers. If mass murder was not new to the Nazis at this point, the sheer magnitude and intended thoroughness of the Final Solution was.

The solution was not self-evident, and it took time to conceive, staff, construct, and set in motion the deportation and death-camp system. When that system was finally ready in the spring of 1942, the military and political circumstances out of which the Final Solution had been born had long been altered. Nonetheless the policy remained unchanged. The readiness of military officers to shoot Jews under the rationalization of military necessity; the availability of technological stopgap devices such as the gas van, initially designed to lighten the psychological burden of the firing-squad killers in the east but now pressed into service as an interim measure to get the murder of European Jews underway; the pressure from local Germans to have their province cleared of Jews first and the zeal with which they competed for that distinction—all these factors helped to create a continuity and momentum behind the killing process from which there was no turning back. The Final Solution may eventually have become a routine procedure—political and logistical preparation, concentration, deportation, gassing or extermination through labor, and disposal of the corpses and property—in which men just followed orders and did their jobs. But it emerged out of a series of decisions and initiatives made not only by Hitler but also by numerous "little men" who, like Sergeant Seith, were eager to do "more than their duty."

Notes

INTRODUCTION

1. Zentrale Stelle der Landesjustizverwaltungen Ludwigsburg, USA Film 1, Frame 90, Seith to Rediess, 8 September 1940.

2. Cited in Adalbert Rückerl, *NS-Vernichtungslager im Spiegel deutscher Strafprozesse: Belzec, Sobibor, Treblinka, Chelmno* (Munich, 1977), pp. 256–57.

3. Investigation by German judicial authorities could establish no causal link. *Ibid.*, p. 257.

4. *Nazi Conspiracy and Aggression*, VII, p. 753 (Document L-3). Because this particular document was of private origin, it was not submitted in evidence to the International Military Tribunal. Two other versions of the speech (Documents 798-PS and 1014-PS) were found in the OKW files. The language there is more circumspect: "Destruction of Poland in the foreground. The aim is the elimination of living forces, not the arrival at a certain line." *Trial of the Major War Criminals before the International Military Tribunal*, II, pp. 286–91.

5. For the political dynamic behind bureaucratic involvement in Nazi Jewish policy, see Christopher R. Browning, "The Government Experts," *The Holocaust: Ideology, Bureaucracy, and Genocide. The San Jose Papers* (New York, 1980), pp. 183–97.

6. Manfred Messerschmidt, "Völkerrecht und 'Kriegsnotwendigkeit' in den deutschen militärischen Tradition seit den Einigungskriegen," *German Studies Review* VI/2 (May 1983), pp. 237–69; Konrad Kwiet, "Zur historiographischen Behandlung der Judenverfolgung im Dritten Reich," *Militärgeschichtliche Mitteilungen* (1980/1), pp. 167–68.

7. Christian Streit, *Keine Kameraden. Die Wehrmacht und die sowjetischen Kriegsgefangenen 1941–1945* (Stuttgart, 1978), p. 10.

1. THE DECISION CONCERNING THE FINAL SOLUTION

1. Martin Broszat, "Hitler und die Genesis der 'Endlösung.' Aus Anlass der Thesen von David Irving," *Vierteljahrshefte für Zeitgeschichte* 25/4 (1977), p. 753.

2. Tim Mason, "Intention and Explanation: A Current Controversy about the Interpretation of National Socialism," *Der Führerstaat: Mythos und Realität*, ed. by Gerhard Hirschfeld and Lothar Kettenacker (Stuttgart, 1981), pp. 21–40.

3. For the intentionalist view, see Karl Dietrich Bracher, "Tradition und Revolution in Nationalsozialismus," *Hitler, Deutschland und die Mächte,* ed. by Manfred Funke (Düsseldorf, 1978), pp. 17–29; and "The Role of Hitler: Perspectives of Interpretation," *Fascism: A Reader's Guide,* ed. by Walter Laqueur (Berkeley, 1976), pp. 211–28. Klaus Hildebrand, "Monokratie oder Polykratie? Hitlers Herrschaft und das Dritte Reich," *Der Führerstaat,* pp. 43–70; and *Das Dritte Reich* (Munich, 1979).

For the functionalists, see Martin Broszat, "Soziale Motivation und Führer-Bindung im Nationalsozialismus," *Vierteljahrshefte für Zeitgeschichte* 18/4 (1970), pp. 392–409; and *The Hitler State: The Foundation and Development of the Internal Structure of the Third Reich* (London, 1981). Hans Mommsen, "National Socialism," *Marxism, Communism, and Western Society,* ed. by C. D. Kernig (New York, 1973), VI, pp. 65–74; "Hitlers Stellung im nationalsozialistischen Herrschaftssystem," *Der Führerstaat,* pp. 43–70; and "National Socialism—Continuity and Change," *Fascism: A Reader's Guide,* pp. 179–210.

4. Lucy Dawidowicz, *The War against the Jews* (New York, 1975), especially pp. 150–63. The psychohistorians also support the 1919 date. See Robert Waite, *The Psychopathic God* (New York, Signet Edition, 1978), and Rudolph Binion, *Hitler and the Germans* (New York, 1976).

5. Helmut Krausnick, "The Persecution of the Jews," *Anatomy of the SS State* (New York, 1968). Andreas Hillgruber: *Hitlers Strategie: Politik und Kriegsführung 1940–41* (Frankfurt, 1965); "Die Endlösung und das deutsche Ostimperium als Kernstück des rassenideologischen Programms des Nationalsozialismus," *Vierteljahrshefte für Zeitgeschichte,* XX/2 (1972), pp. 133–53; and "Die Ideologisch-dogmatische Grundlage der nationalsozialistischen Politik der Ausrottung der Juden in den besetzten Gebieten der Sowjetunion und ihre Durchführung 1941–44," *German Studies Review,* II/2 (1979), pp. 263–96. Eberhard Jäckel, *Hitler's Weltanschauung: A Blueprint for Power* (Middletown, Conn., 1972). Karl Dietrich Bracher, *The German Dictatorship* (New York, 1966), especially pp. 366–68. Ernst Nolte, *The Three Faces of Fascism* (New York, 1966), also stressed the ideological factor.

6. Gerald Fleming, *Hitler und die Endlösung. "Es ist des Führers Wunsch . . ."* (Wiesbaden and Munich, 1982), pp. 13–14, 25–27. Sarah Gordon, *Hitler, Germans, and the "Jewish Question"* (Princeton, 1984), p. 136.

7. Karl Schleunes, *The Twisted Road to Auschwitz* (Urbana, Ill., 1970). Uwe Dietrich Adam, *Judenpolitik im Dritten Reich* (Düsseldorf, 1972).

8. Raul Hilberg, *The Destruction of the European Jews* (Chicago, 1961), pp. 640, 18, 770.

9. *Ibid.,* pp. 4, 640.

10. Eberhard Jäckel, *Hitlers Weltanschauung* (Revised and Expanded Edition: Stuttgart, 1981), p. 73. In an as yet unpublished paper ("Hitler und der Mord an den europäischen Juden im Zweiten Weltkrieg: Ein Beitrag zur Frage der Entschlussbildung") presented in Warsaw in April 1983, Eberhard Jäckel has recently proposed analyzing the decision-making process for the Final Solution by the comparative method. He divides the more amply documented stages of Hitler's foreign-policy decision making into the following stages: conception, long-term planning, internal preparation, opportunistic detour, decision for implementation, operative preparations, and final orders. He hypothesizes that similar stages probably characterized Hitler's decision-making process on Jewish policy. He concludes that although Hitler conceived of the extermination of the Jews in the 1920s, the historian should not seek a single date or decision by which this conception was transformed into policy. Rather, the Final Solution emerged out of a long-term political process, albeit one which was decisively dominated by the continuity of Hitler's intentions.

11. Hillgruber and Krausnick in particular, but also Robert Kempner, *Eichmann und Komplizen* (Zurich, 1961), p. 96–97. An early 1941 date is advocated by Leon Poliakov, *Harvest of Hate* (London, 1958), p. 110.

12. Hilberg, *The Destruction of the European Jews,* p. 177.

13. Adam, *Judenpolitik im Dritten Reich,* pp. 303–13.

14. David Irving, *Hitler's War* (London, 1977).

15. Martin Broszat, "Hitler und die Genesis der 'Endlösung.' Aus Anlass der Thesen von David Irving," *Vierteljahrshefte für Zeitgeschichte,* 25/4 (October 1977), pp. 739–75. For other critiques of Irving, see Bradley Smith, "Two Alibis for the Inhumanities: A. R. Butz, *The Hoax of the Twentieth Century,* and David Irving, *Hitler's War," German Studies Review,* I/3 (October 1978), pp. 327–35; Charles Sydnor, "The selling of Adolf Hitler: David Irving's *Hitler's War," Central European History* XII (June 1979), pp. 182–85; Eberhard Jäckel, "Hitler und der Mord an den europäischen Juden," *Frankfurter Allgemeine Zeitung,* August 25, 1977, p. 17, and "Noch Einmal: Irving, Hitler und der Judenmord," *Frankfurter Allgemeine Zeitung,* June 22, 1978, p. 23. Gerald Fleming's *Hitler und die Endlösung* also takes direct aim at Irving.

16. Christopher R. Browning, "Zur Genesis der 'Endlösung'. Eine Antwort an Martin Broszat," *Vierteljahrshefte für Zeitgeschichte,* 29/1 (January 1981), pp. 97–109. Kurt Pätzold, "Von der Vertreibung zum Genozid. Zu den Ursachen, Triebkräften und Bedingungen der antijüdischen Politik des faschistischen deutschen Imperialismus," *Faschismusforschung: Positionen, Probleme, Polemik* (Köln, 1980), pp. 181–208. Wolfgang Scheffler, "Zur Entstehungsgeschichte der 'Endlösung,'" *Aus Politik und Zeitgeschichte. Beilage zur Wochenzeitung Das Parlement,* B 43/82, November 30, 1982, pp. 3–10. Eberhard Jäckel, "Hitler und der Mord an den europäischen Juden im Zweiten Weltkrieg: Ein Beitrag zur Frage der Entschlussbildung," to be published in the proceedings of the Warsaw Conference on Nazi Crimes against Humanity in Poland and Europe 1939–1945, April 14–17, 1983. Gerald Fleming, *Hitler und die Endlösung,* 56–59, and Sarah Gordon, *Hitler, Germans, and the "Jewish Question,"* pp. 141–42, 147, date Hitler's orders to the summer of 1941.

17. Christian Streit, *Keine Kameraden: Die Wehrmacht und die sowjetischen Kriegsgefangenen 1941–1945* (Stuttgart, 1978), pp. 127, 356. Alfred Streim, *Die Behandlung sowjetischer Kriegsgefangener im "Fall Barabarossa"* (Heidelberg and Karlsruhe, 1981), pp. 74–93.

18. Helmut Krausnick and Hans-Heinrich Wilhelm, *Die Truppe des Weltanschauungskrieges: Die Einsatzgruppen der Sicherheitspolizei und des SD 1938–1942* (Stuttgart, 1981), pp. 159–64, 533–39.

19. Sebastian Haffner, *The Meaning of Hitler* (New York, 1979), 142–43.

20. Shlomo Aronson, "Die Dreifache Falle: Hitlers Judenpolitik, die Alliierten und die Juden," *Vierteljahrshefte für Zeitgeschichte,* 32/1 (January 1984), pp. 28–65.

21. Hans Mommsen, "Die Realisierung des Utopischen: Die 'Endlösung der Judenfrage' im 'Dritten Reich',," *Geschichte und Gesellschaft,* IX/3 (Autumn 1983), pp. 381–420. The term "weak dictator" is Mommsen's own from earlier writings, but does not appear in this particular article.

22. *Hitler's Secret Conversations,* ed. by H. R. Trevor Roper (New York, Signet Edition, 1961), pp. 238, 260. Entries of January 23 and 28, 1942.

23. Broszat, "Soziale Motivation und Führer-Bindung des Nationalsozialismus."

24. Mason, "Intention and Explanation," p. 33.

25. For psychological assessments of Hitler's anti-Semitism, see Robert Waite, *The Psychopathic God,* and Rudolph Binion, *Hitler and the Germans.*
For anti-Semitism and Hitler's ideology, see Jäckel, *Hitler's Weltanschauung,* and the articles of Andreas Hillgruber, note 5, above. The most graphic of Hitler's murderous fantasies is cited in Waite, p. 440: "As soon as I have the power, I shall have gallows after gallows erected, for example in Munich on the Marienplatz. . . . Then the Jews will be hanged one after another, and they will stay hanging until they stink. They will stay hanging as long as hygienically possible. As soon as they are untied, then the next group will follow and that will continue until the last Jew in Munich is exterminated. Exactly the same

procedure will be followed in other cities until Germany is cleansed of Jews!" This dates from 1922.

26. For instance, Hitler's support for continuing the Haavara agreement despite considerable internal opposition, and his support of Schacht's negotiations over Ribbentrop's objections, as well as his backing of Göring, Himmler, and Heydrich over Goebbels and his encouragement to the Madagascar planners. Christopher R. Browning, *The Final Solution and the German Foreign Office* (New York, 1978), pp. 14, 17–18, 38, 41.

27. Dawidowicz, *The War against the Jews,* pp. 93, 158. Bracher, *The German Dictatorship,* p. 366.

28. Helmut Krausnick and Hans-Heinrich Wilhelm, *Die Truppe des Weltanschauungskrieges* (Stuttgart, 1981); Christian Streit, *Keine Kameraden* (Stuttgart, 1978); Andreas Hillgruber, *Hitlers Strategie: Politik und Kriegsführung 1940–1* (Frankfurt, 1965); Hans-Adolf Jacobsen, "The Kommissarbefehl and Mass Executions of Soviet Prisoners of War," *Anatomy of the SS State,* pp. 505–35; Helmut Krausnick, "Kommissarbefehl and 'Gerichtsbarkeitserlass Barbarossa' in Neuen Sicht," *Vierteljahrshefte für Zeitgeschichte* 25/4 (1977), pp. 682–738; Jürgen Förster, "The Wehrmacht and the War of Extermination against the Soviet Union," *Yad Vashem Studies* XIV (1981), pp. 7–34, and *Das Deutsche Reich und der Zweite Weltkrieg,* IV: *Der Angriff auf die Sowjetunion* (Stuttgart, 1983), pp. 413–47, 1030–88.

29. See footnotes 17 and 18. This debate was also vigorously pursued at the Stuttgart conference on "The Murder of the European Jews in the Second World War: Decision-making process and realization," May 3–5, 1984. The proceedings will be published by the Deutsche Verlags-Anstalt.

30. Streim, *Die Behandlung sowjetischer Kriegsgefangenen im "Fall Barbarossa,"* pp. 75–6, 81, 85.

31. Krausnick, *Die Truppe des Weltanschauungskrieges,* pp. 160–61.

32. Streim, *Die Behandlung sowjetischer Kriegsgefangenen im "Fall Barbarossa,"* pp. 83–84, 89.

33. Krausnick, *Die Truppe des Weltanschauungskrieges,* 162–65.

34. Streim, *Die Behandlung sowjetischer Kriegsfegangenen im "Fall Barabarossa,"* p. 93.

35. Landgericht Köln, 24 Ks 1/52, Bd. III, 747–55 (testimony of Erwin Schulz, 3 February 1953).

36. Wilhelm, *Die Truppe des Weltanschauungskrieges,* pp. 535–36, 539.

37. L-180 (Stahlecker report) in *Trials of the Major War Criminals before the International Military Tribunal* (Nürnburg, 1947–49), XXVII, pp. 687, 702. Hereafter cited as IMT.

38. Cited in Krausnick and Wilhelm, *Die Truppe des Weltanschauungskrieges,* p. 534. "Das Ziel, das dem Einsatzkommando 2 von Anfang an vorschwebte, war eine radikale Lösung des Judenproblems durch die Exekution aller Juden."

39. Streit has argued for the latter interpretation, i.e., the readiness of the army to cooperate in Hitler's *Ausrottungspolitik* in itself contributed to radicalizing this policy. *Keine Kameraden,* p. 126. Hillgruber, on the other hand, has argued that the attacks upon Russia, Bolshevism, and the Jews were inseparable in Hitler's mind.

40. Krausnick and Wilhelm, *Die Truppe des Weltanschauungskrieges,* p. 137.

41. Cited in Kempner, *Eichmann und Komplizen,* p. 97. "Was ich heute nicht niederschreiben will, aber nie vergessen werde."

42. Cited in Michael Marrus and Robert Paxton, *Vichy France and the Jews* (New York, 1981), p. 10.

43. Browning, *The Final Solution and the German Foreign Office,* pp. 43–44, 46.

44. Hilberg, *The Destruction of the European Jews,* p. 177, and remarks at the Stuttgart

conference on "The Murder of the European Jews in the Second World War: Decision-making and realization," May 3–5, 1984.

45.   710-PS, in IMT, XXVI, pp. 266–67.

46.   Broszat, "Hitler und die Genesis der 'Endlösung.' Aus Anlass der Thesen von David Irving," p. 747; Adam, *Judenpolitik im Dritten Reich,* pp. 308–9.

47.   Adolph Eichmann, *Ich Adolf Eichmann. Ein historischer Zeugenbericht,* ed. by Dr. Rudolf Aschenauer (Leoni am Starnberger See: Druffel-Verlag, 1980), p. 479. Bundesarchiv Koblenz, All. proz. 6/199, "Meine Memoiren," manuscript pp. 112–13. As Eberhard Jäckel has recently noted, according to Göring's appointment book Heydrich had scheduled a one-hour visit on the early evening of July 31, 1941, during which time the authorization could have been submitted for Göring's signature. The fact that the document was not written on Göring's letterhead but rather on a plain sheet of paper, Jäckel notes, further strengthens the suspicion that it was drafted by Heydrich. Eberhard Jäckel, "Die Entschlussbildung als Historisches Problem," presented to the Stuttgart conference on "The Murder of the European Jews in the Second World War: Decision-making and realization," May 3–5, 1984.

48.   National Archives, Wi/ID 1420 (old Wi/ID 2.139), "Anlage zu: Verb. St. d. OKW/Wi Rü Amt beim Reichsmarschall v. 14 August 1941." I am grateful to Professor Dr. Helmut Krausnick for sending me a copy of this document.

49.   Politisches Archiv des Auswärtigen Amtes (hereafter cited as PA), Inland IIg 177, Heydrich to Ribbentrop, 24 June 1940 (NG-25886-J). Browning, *The Final Solution and the German Foreign Office,* p. 38.

50.   3868-PS, in IMT, XXXIII, p. 277.

51.   IMT, XI, pp. 396–422. Testimony of 15 April 1946.

52.   Rudolf Höss, *Commandant of Auschwitz* (New York: Popular Library Edition, 1959), pp. 135–38 and 173–75.

53.   This does not include the first gas vans used by *Sonderkommando* Lange in euthanasia operations in 1940, which utilized bottled carbon monoxide, not exhaust gas. See chapter 3.

54.   "Eichmann tells his own damning story," *Life Magazine* 49/22 (28 November 1960).

55.   All these materials can be found in the Budesarchiv Koblenz. Interrogations: All. Proz. 6/1-6; the handwritten "Meine Memoiren": All. Proz. 6/119; and Eichmann's notes to his attorney: All. Proz. 6/169. Parts of the interrogations have now been published by Farrar, Straus and Giroux, New York, as *Eichmann Interrogated.*

56.   *Ich Adolf Eichmann. Ein historischer Zeugenbericht,* ed. by Dr. Ruldolf Aschenauer.

57.   H. G. Adler, *Theresienstadt 1941–1945* (Tübingen, 1960, 2nd edition), pp. 720–22.

58.   Zentrale Stelle der Landesjustizverwaltungen Ludwigsburg (hereafter cited as ZStL): 8 AR-Z 252/59, vol. I, pp. 24–31.

59.   PA, Inland II A/B 47/1, Eichmann to D III, 28 August 1941.

60.   PA, Inland IIg 194, Rademacher marginalia, 13 September 1941, on Benzler letter of 12 September 1941.

61.   PA, Pol.Abt. III 246, Luther memoranda of 13 and 17 October 1941.

62.   *Akten zur Deutschen Aussenpolitik, 1918–1945* (hereafter cited as ADAP), Series D, XIII, Part 2 (Göttingen, 1970), pp. 570–72.

63.   PA, Inland II A/B 59/3, Wurm to Rademacher, 23 October 1941.

64.   NO-365, NO-996, and NO-997.

65.   The difficulty in procurement and production of gas vans in the desired numbers is confirmed by testimony in the gas-van trial (Landgericht Hannover 2 Ks 2/65: Strafsache gegen Pradel und Wentritt) and by surviving documents of the automotive section (II D 3) of the RSHA (BA, R 58/871). See Chapter 3.

66. H. G. Adler, *Theresienstadt 1941–1945*, pp. 720–22. The day following Heydrich's meeting in Prague, Stahlecker informed the *Generalkommissar* of Latvia, Dr. Drechsler, that a concentration camp near Riga was to be set up for Jews from the Reich and Protectorate. On November 8 *Sturmbannführer* Lange of *Einsatzgruppe* A confirmed that 25,000 Jews were coming to the new camp at Salspils near Riga and another 25,000 to Minsk. When Dr. Trempedach of the RK Ostland wrote to Berlin to urge that the transports be stopped, Dr. Leibbrandt of the *Ostministerium* replied that there was no cause for worry since the Jews would be sent "further east." Hilberg, *Destruction of the European Jews*, p. 232.

67. 2718-PS, in IMT, XXXI, p. 84.

68. 126-EC, in IMT, XXXVI, pp. 141, 145.

69. National Archives, Wi/ID 1420 (old Wi/ID 2.139), "Anlage zu: Verb. St. D. OKW/Wi Rü Amt beim Reichsmarschall v. 14 August 1941."

70. PA, Inland II g 177, Reichssicherheitshauptamt Madagaskar Projekt.

71. ZStL, IV 402 AR-Z 37/58; (Landgericht Frankfurt, 4 Ks 2/63, Urteil), pp. 82, 242; Sonderband VI, 970 (testimony of Hans Stark). *Hefte von Auschwitz*, III, "Kalendarium 1942."

72. ZStL: V 203 AR-Z 69/59, Judgment in the Chelmno process, Landgericht Bonn 8 Ks 2/63, pp. 24 and 92; and 203 AR-Z 69/59, IV, pp. 624–43, and VI, pp. 961–89 (testimony of Walter Burmeister). Part of Burmeister's testimony has now been published in *National-sozialistische Massentötungen durch Giftgas*, ed. by Eugen Kogen, Hermann Langbein, and Adalbert Rückerl, et al. (Frankfurt, 1983), pp. 113–14.

73. ZStL, 203 AR-Z 69/59, VII, pp. 1288–93 (testimony of Konrad S.) The testimony of four other *Volksdeutschen*—Nelli L., Herbert W., Adele F., and Erhard M., also in volume VII—corroborates Konrad S.'s testimony. Further Chelmno testimony pertinent to this question has now been published in *Nationalsozialistische Massentötungen durch Giftgas*, pp. 118–21.

74. ZStL, 8 AR-Z 252/59, IX, pp. 1680–87 (testimony of Josef Oberhauser of 12 December 1962). Earlier testimony of Oberhauser was less forthcoming, and even this testimony lacks credibility for events after March 1942, when it appears that Oberhauser was making a minimal confession as part of a tacit plea-bargaining arrangement for a minimal sentence. However, his testimony on pre-March 1942 events, that did not involve any of the criminal charges against him, was more detailed and convincing.

75. *Ibid.*, VI: testimony of Ludwik O., Eustachy I., Mieczyslaw K., Stanislaw Kozak, Edward L., Tadeusz M., Michal K., Maria B., Jan G., Viktor S., Alojzy B., Franciszek B., and Edward F. Part of the Kozak testimony has now been published in *Nationalsozialis-tische Massentötungen durch Giftgas*, pp. 152–53.

76. *Ibid.*, V, pp. 974–75.

77. Landgericht Hannover 2 Ks 2/65, III, pp. 64–68. ZStL, 8 AR-Z 252/59, V, pp. 981–89.

78. See chapter 3.

79. Browning, *The Final Solution and the German Foreign Office*, pp. 72–76.

80. Felix Kersten, *The Kersten Memoirs 1940–45* (New York, 1957), p. 119.

81. PA, Pol. XIII, VAA Berichte, text of Rosenberg speech of 18 November 1941. T 120/270/339/198808-21.

82. 1517-PS, in IMT, XXVII, p. 270.

83. 3666-PS, in IMT, XXXII, p. 437.

84. *Das Diensttagebuch des deutschen Generalgouverneurs in Polen 1939–1945*, ed. by Werner Präg and Wolfgang Jacobmayer (Stuttgart, 1975), pp. 457–58; IMT, XII, pp. 68–69; Hilberg, *The Destruction of the European Jews*, p. 263.

85. NG-2586 C. Photocopy in Kempner, *Eichmann und Komplizen*, pp. 127–28.

86. ADAP, E, I, pp. 267–76. Photocopy in Kempner, *Eichmann und Komplizen*, pp. 133–47.

87. Bernd Nellessen, *Der Prozess von Jerusalem* (Düsseldorf, 1964), p. 206.

88. Bernhard Lösener, "Als Rassereferent im Reichsministerium des Innern," *Vierteljahrshefte für Zeitgeschichte* IX/3 (1961), p. 303; Broszat, "Hitler und die Genesis der 'Endlösung.' Aus Anlass der Thesen von David Irving," p. 750.

89. PA, Inland II g 194, Rademacher marginalia of 13 September on Benzler letter of 12 September 1941.

90. H. G. Adler, *Der Verwaltete Mensch: Studien zur Deportation der Juden aus Deutschland* (Tübingen, 1974), pp. 173–77.

91. Adler, *Theresienstadt*, pp. 720–22.

92. In addition to Himmler's assurances to Greiser and Eichmann's statement to that effect recorded by Wetzel (NO-365), see note 66 above.

93. Lösener, "Als Rassereferent im Reichsministerium des Innern," pp. 303–5; Adam, *Judenpolitik im Dritten Reich*, p. 337.

94. *The Goebbels Diaries 1942–3*, ed. by Louis Lochner (Garden City, N.Y., 1948), pp. 115–16.

95. Browning, *The Final Solution and the German Foreign Office*, pp. 79–81.

96. *The Goebbels Diaries 1942–3*, pp. 147–48.

97. Gerald Fleming has diligently assembled the various Himmler references in this regard in *Hitler und die Endlösung*.

98. Browning, *The Final Solution and the German Foreign Office*.

99. See note 22 above. Also the entry for 25 October 1941 (pp. 108–9).

2. WEHRMACHT REPRISAL POLICY AND THE MURDER OF THE MALE JEWS IN SERBIA

1. Christian Streit, *Keine Kameraden. Die Wehrmacht und die sowjetischen Kriegsgefangenen 1941–1945* (Stuttgart, 1978); Helmut Karusnick und Hans-Heinrich Wilhelm, *Die Truppe des Weltanschauungskrieges* (Stuttgart, 1981); and Jürgen Förster, "The Wehrmacht and the War of Extermination against the Soviet Union," *Yad Vashem Studies* XIV (1981), pp. 7–34, and *Das Deutsche Reich und der Zweite Weltkrieg*, IV: *Der Angriff auf die Sowjetunion* (Stuttgart, 1983), pp. 413–47, 1030–88.

2. In Case VII against the Wehrmacht's Balkan generals, the American military tribunal in Nürnberg ruled that German reprisal policy as practiced in Serbia constituted a war crime in itself and therefore made no effort to distinguish between Wehrmacht executions of Serbs and Jews. The East German scholars Norbert Müller and Martin Zöller likewise made no distinction in their study, "Okkupationsverbrechen der faschistischen Wehrmacht gegenüber der serbischen Bevölkerung im Herbst 1941," *Zeitschrift für Militärgeschichte*, IX, (1970) pp. 704–15. Following the pretrial investigation of a German officer charged with shooting Jews in Serbia, a postwar German court ruled that Wehrmacht reprisal policy had not been criminal, even when the victims were Jews. It ruled that the army had been duped by the SS into shooting Jews unwittingly. As no "base" *(niedrige)*, i.e., racial, motive was therefore involved on the part of army personnel, they had not committed murder as defined by German law and charges were dropped. Another German court investigating a similar case seized the precedent with alacrity and halted its own investigation, and other pending cases were also not taken up. Landgericht Kassel, 3 Js 11/66, Ermittlungsverfahren gegen Walther Liepe, pp. 22–30 (Zentrale Stelle der Landesjustizverwaltungen, Ludwigsburg, to Landgericht Kassel, 19 January 1966) and pp. 63–66 (Einstellungsverfügung).

3. Edmund Veesenmayer, Ribbentrop's roving ambassador, sarcastically referred to them as the "seven or five kings of Serbia." NG-2905.

4. Bundesarchiv-Militärarchiv Freiburg (hereafter cited as BA-MA): RW 40/7, conference of 22 June 1941; RH 26-104/3, entries of 13 and 14 July 1941; RH 26-104/7, Schröder to 65th Corps, 22 June 1941; RW 14/184, Turner report, 10 July 1941. Paul Hehn, *The German Struggle Against Yugoslav Guerrillas in World War II. German Counter-Insurgency in Yugoslavia 1941–1943* (New York, 1979), p. 20.

5. Landgericht Köln 24 Ks 1/52, Verfahren gegen Emanuel Schäfer, II, pp. 397–98 (testimony of Alexander F.). BA-MA, RW 40/4: entry of 5 July 1941; and Anlage 33, report of 22 July 1941 (NOKW-1091). NO-2942 (report of Chef der Sipo-SD, 19 July 1941). American Military Tribunal, Case VII (hereafter cited as AMT VII), transcript, p. 917 (testimony of Georg Kiessel).

6. BA-MA, RH 26-104/8, Anlage 156, Verfügung über Vorbeugungs- und Sühnemassnahmen, Militärbefehlshaber in Serbien, Verwaltungsstab, Tgb. Nr. 144/41.

7. BA-MA, RW 40/4, Anlage 61, Ehrmann report, 1 August 1941. Politisches Archiv des Auswärtigen Amtes, Bonn (hereafter cited as PA), Staatssekretär-Jugoslawien, Bd. 3, Benzler to Foreign Office, 1 August 1941. NOKW-1661 (Kiessel to Tippelskirch, 9 August 1941) and NOKW-551 (OKW daily report of 11 August 1941).

8. BA-MA, RW 40/4: entry of 22 July 1941; and Anlage 33, Gravenhorst to 65th corps, 21 July 1941.

9. BA-MA, RW 40/4: entries of 24 and 29 July 1941; and Anlage 48, List to Danckelmann, 29 July 1941.

10. PA, Staatssekretär-Jugoslawien, Bd. 3, Benzler to Foreign Office, 23 July 1941. BA-MA: RW 40/4, Anlage 35, Kiessel to List, 23 July 1941; RH 26-104/9, Anlage 116, Jost report, 30 July 1941, and Anlage 179g, Borowski to 65th corps, 9 August 1941.

11. BA-MA, RW 40/5: Anlage 1, Danckelmann to List, 2 August 1941; and Anlage 2, Danckelmann to OKH, 3 August 1941.

12. BA-MA, RW 40/5: entry of 4 August 1941; Anlage 42, memorandum for Veesenmayer; Anlage 22, OKW to Danckelmann, 9 August 1941; and entry of 16 August 1941.

13. BA-MA: RW 40/5, entry of 9 August 1941; RH 26-104/9, Anlage 180, Stobbe to 704th division, 7 August 1941; RH 26-114/3, August summary.

14. PA: Staatssekretär-Jugoslawien, Bd. 3, Benzler to Foreign Office, 23 July and 1 August 1941; Inland IIg 401, Benzler to Foreign Office, 8 August 1941. BA-MA: RW 40/4, Anlage 45, report of Feldkommandantur 816 for 12–27 July 1941, and Anlage 59, Ic report of Picht for July; 14 749/18, reports of Wehrmachtverbindungsstelle, 31 July and 8 August 1941 (NOKW-1114).

15. BA-MA, 14 749/18, conference of 21 August 1941.

16. BA-MA, RW 40/5: Anlagen 47 and 48, daily reports of 15 and 16 August 1941. AMT VII, transcript, p. 918.

17. Hehn, *German Struggle,* pp. 28–29.

18. BA-MA, 40411/6, Bader report of 23 August 1941.

19. BA-MA, 40411/7, Bader to List, 28 August 1941.

20. PA: Staatssekretär-Jugoslawien, Bd. 3, Benzler to Foreign Office, 23 July, 8 August and 12 August 1941; and Inland II A/B 65/4, Benzler to Foreign Office, 14 August 1941. BA-MA: RW 40/4, Anlage 35, Kiessel to List, 23 July 1941, Anlage 45, report of FK 816 for 12–27 July 1941, and Anlage 59, Ic report of Picht for July; RW 40/5, Anlage 1, Danckelmann to List, 2 August 1941, and Anlage 2, Danckelmann to OKH, 3 August 1941, and Anlage 40, Danckelmann to OKW, 14 August 1941; RW 40/184, Turner report, 10 July 1941; RW 40/185, Turner report, 10 August 1941.

21. PA, Staatssekretär-Jugoslawien, Bd. 3, Benzler to Foreign Office, 27 and 28 August

1941. BA-MA: RW 40/186, Turner report, 6 September 1941; RW 40/5, entry for 2 August 1941, Anlage 103, Turner to FK, KK, 29 August 1941, Anlage 111, report of Ic Fetz, 21–31 August 1941, Anlage 114, report of Ia Kogard for August 1941. Bundesarchiv Koblenz (hereafter cited as BA), NS 19/1730, Danckelmann to List, 3 September 1941. Hehn, *German Struggle*, p. 28.

22. Hehn, *German Struggle*, pp. 29–30, 34–35.

23. BA-MA, RW 40/13, List to OKW, OKH, 8 September 1941.

24. Hehn, *German Struggle*, p. 30.

25. BA-MA: 14 749/5, Anlage 58, List to Danckelmann and Bader, 4 September 1941 (NOKW-453); RW 40/11, Anlage 7, List to Danckelmann, 5 September 1941 (NOKW-625).

26. On List, see (a) his testimony before the American Military Tribunal, transcript, p. 3148 ff., p. 3321 ff., p. 9605 ff.; (b) his pretrial interrogations, Nürnberg Staatsarchiv (hereafter cited as NStA), Rep. 502, VI, L 65; (c) the account of his chief of staff, Hermann Foertsch, Institut für Zeitgeschichte, Zz 37; and (d) the List Defense Documents, NStA, Rep. 501, VII, Le, vol. 2–10.

27. NStA, List Defense Documents 159 (affidavit of Hans Kliemann) and 164a (affidavit of Hans Schweiger). According to X. Switlik (List Defense Document 163), List also attended and supported the Athens Philharmonic concerts.

28. NOKW-1621 (commanding general of 14th army to all commanders, 18 September 1939).

29. NStA, List Defense Documents 47 (affidavit of Otto Wöhler) and 21 (affidavit of Alfred Grün).

30. NStA, List Defense Document 35 (affidavit of Angelo Roncalli).

31. NStA, List Defense Documents 23 (affidavit of Franz Halder) and 134 (affidavit of Konrad Rudolf).

32. On two later occasions List explicitly referred to these guidelines, once in fact telling the OKW that they contained the measures he deemed necessary. (NStA, Rep. 502, VI, L 65, interrogation of 21 July 1947. BA-MA: RW 40/13, List to OKW, OKH, 8 September 41; and 17 729.4, List to Böhme, 18 September 1941.) List's other claim at Nürnberg, that he had protested the OKW order to hang all insurgents, is supported by documentary evidence, however. On 29 August 1941, the OKW reiterated its order that insurgents be hanged, not shot. (BA-MA, RW 40/5, entry of 29 August 1941.) On 3 September 1941, Warlimont informed Foertsch, then back from Greece, that his chief had just requested that special instructions of the OKW in regard to the treatment of insurgents be canceled. This request was supported by Warlimont, who noted that Hitler took an extraordinary interest in the insurgency. Such orders from the OKW were not to limit or restrict the responsibility of the local commanders, Warlimont advised, but merely to keep them informed of the special interests and wishes of the Führer! BA-MA, 14 749/5, Anlage 64a, Warlimont to Foertsch, 3 September 1941. This letter may corroborate List's contention that he protested on this occasion, but it also shows that the OKW was passing on such orders to placate Hitler and viewed them as advice and information which they intimated to lower authorities were not intended to be enforced literally.

33. AMT VII, transcript, pp. 3427–9.

34. BA-MA, RW 40/186, Turner report, 6 September 1941.

35. Hehn, *German Struggle*, p. 31.

36. PA, Staatssekretär-Jugoslawien, Bd. 4, Benzler to Foreign Office, 12 September 1941. BA-MA, RW 40/11: Anlage 31, Danckelmann to 65th corps, 12 September 1941; and Anlage 33, daily report of 12 September 1941.

37. Hehn, *German Struggle*, pp. 37–39. AMT VII, transcript, p. 4158 (Foertsch testimony).

38. On Böhme, see NOKW-876, 1560, and 1041; and NStA, Rep. 502, VI B 110.

39. BA-MA: 14 749/4, Anlage 68, List to OKW, 13 September 1941 (NOKW-1424), and entry of 14 September 1941; 14 749/5, Anlage 70, OKW to List, 14 September 41; and RH 2/ 680, Hitler to List, 16 September 1941 (NOKW-1492).

40. BA-MA, 17 729.4: Anlage 11, Kewisch report, 21 September 1941; and Anlage 17, Turner to Böhme, 21 September 1941 (NOKW-892).

41. BA-MA, 17 729.4: Anlage 20, Böhme order of 22 September 1941 (NOKW-183); Anlage 22, Böhme order of 23 September 1941 (NOKW-194); 17 729.9, Anlage 17, Pemsel to Turner and 342nd division, 27 September 1941 (NOKW-193); Anlage 31, Böhme order and message to troops, 25 September 1941 (NOKW-1048).

42. BA-MA: RW 40/11, Anlage 44, daily report of 14 September 1941, and Anlage 52, daily report of 16 September 1941; 17 729.2, entry of 25 September 1941.

43. BA-MA: 17 729.4, Anlage 28, Böhme to List, 25 September 1941, and Anlage 45, 10-day report, 1 October 1941; 17 729.2, entry of 27 September 1941; 40411/1, Anlage 13, Böhme to List, 28 September 1941.

44. BA-MA, 17 729.2, entry of 29 September 1941.

45. M. Jovanovic, "Wir Packen, Wir Auspacken. Tragniča Sudbina Jevreja-Isbeglica U Sapcu 1941," *Zbornik* 4 (1979), pp. 245–79. Hinghofer had ordered that the evacuation be carried out "with the greatest severity and without false sense of pity." *(mit allergrösster Schärfe und ohne falsch verstandenes Mitleid)* BA-MA, 15 365.7, Hinghofer to divisional units, 24 September 1941. The guard, mostly *Volksdeutsche* and Croatians, were reported to have shot many prisoners trying to escape. (BA-MA, 15 365.14, Schuster to Ia, 1 October 1941.)

46. BA-MA, 15 365.7: Krogh to regiments, 29 September 1941, and Ia to IR 699, 28 September 1941.

47. BA-MA: 15 365.7, Schuster note of 2 October, 1941, initialed by Hinghofer; RW 40/ 12, entry of 2 October 1941.

48. BA-MA, 15 365.7, Ia note of 4 October 1941, and order of 5 October 1941. Also on October 3, Hinghofer tightened regulations concerning court-martial shootings; the accused had to be guilty of some form of resistance, not just failing to obey the German orders to report to the collection points. BA-MA, 15 365.7, Abt. III 7/41g, 3 October 1941.

49. BA-MA, 15 365.16, summary for 24 September–9 October 1941.

50. BA-MA: 15 365.3, entry of 7 October 1941; 17 729.4, Anlage 80, Böhme to 342nd division, 7 October 1941.

51. BA-MA: 17 729.2, entries of 2 and 3 October 1941; RH 26-114/3, October summary. AMT VII, transcript, pp. 8433–4 (testimony of Topola Survivor, Johann Kerbler).

52. BA-MA, 17 729.2, entry of 2 October 1941.

53. BA-MA, 17 729.9, Anlage 48, excerpt from Keitel order of 16 September 1941 (NOKW-258). When these guidelines reached Belgrade is unknown, but Böhme's quarter-master, Captain Hans Georg Faulmüller, discussed measures against insurgents for the death or wounding of German soldiers with List's quartermaster on September 26, and possibly was made aware of Keitel's directive at this time. BA-MA, 17 729.8, entry of 26 September 1941.

54. BA-MA, 17 729.8, Anlage 24, Faulmüller draft of order to Turner and 342nd division, 4 October 1941, with Faulmüller marginal note (NOKW-192). On October 8 Faulmüller would be granted jurisdiction over reprisal measures. BA-MA, 17 729.8, entry of 8 October 1941.

55. BA-MA, 17 729.8, Anlage 28, Keitel to List, 28 September 1941 (NOKW-458).
56. BA-MA: 17 729.8, Anlage 28, List to Böhme, 4 October 1941 (NOKW-203); 17 729.2, entry of 5 October 1941.

57.   BA-MA, 17 729.9, Anlage 48, Böhme order, nr. 2848/41g, 10 October 1941. (NOKW-891 and 557).

58.   AMT VII, transcript, p. 3370.

59.   This behavior is not dissimilar to the earlier reaction of professional diplomats of the German Foreign Office in the 1930s who, under the impact of the boycott of German exports and the barrage of foreign criticism of Nazi treatment of the Jews, quickly habituated themselves to the premise that the Jews of the world were Germany's enemy. It was thus both a professional duty and an act of patriotism to defend Nazi Jewish policy abroad and to oppose any softening in this policy as an intolerable sign of vulnerability to foreign pressure. Christopher R. Browning, *The Final Solution and the German Foreign Office* (New York, 1978), pp. 11–22.

60.   M. Jovanovic, "Wir Packen."

61.   Browning, *Final Solution,* pp. 56–59.

62.   Böhme's requests: BA-MA, 17 729.2, entry of 3 October 1941, and 17 729.4, Anlage 66, Böhme to List, 4 October 1941. List's rejections: BA-MA 17 729.4, Anlage 62, List to Böhme, 4 October 1941, and 17 729.2, entry of 6 October 1941. On Zasavica: BA-MA, 17 729.8, entry of 3 October 1941, and 17 729.9, Anlage 30, Pemsel to Turner and Faulmüller, 6 October 1941 (NOKW-262).

63.   That the behavior of the German military in Serbia was not an aberration, given the partisan resistance and their acceptance of the Jew as the enemy, can be seen in the similar response of the German military in France to growing resistance. First, a high percentage of Jews were among the victims of hostage shootings and mass arrests. Then the military threatened the mass deportation of Communists and Jews in retaliation for resistance, which in practice meant the deportation of 1,117 Jews on 27 March 1942, to Auschwitz—the first step in the Final Solution in France. Michael Marrus and Robert Paxton, *Vichy France and the Jews* (New York, 1981), pp. 225–28.

64.   BA-MA, 17 729.9, Anlage 64, Liepe report of 13 October 1941 (NOKW-497). One cover letter was signed by Pemsel, Faulmüller, Turner and Kiessel, so interest was not minimal. A second cover letter on this report notes that further executions would be carried out by the Korps-Nachr. Abt. Pongruber. At least some of Liepe's unit were also involved in a third execution. Landgericht Kassel, 3 Js 11/66, Ermittlungsverfahren gegen Walter Liepe, p. 158 (testimony of Hans A.) and 181 (testimony of Otto W.). The last executions for the Topola ambush may have run well into the month of October, as material collected by Faulmüller for the 10-day report of 30 October 1941 credits the "Höh. Nachr. Fü." with reporting 202 hostage shootings. (BA-MA, 17 729.9, Anlage 10, quartermaster material for 10-day report of 30 October 1941. NOKW-199.) Though the Belgrade victims were predominately Serbian Jews, at least some were refugees, including a former officer of the Hungarian army and one veteran with an Iron Cross. LG Kassel, 3 Js 11/66, p. 159 (testimony of Wilhelm D.) and p. 180 (testimony of Otto W.).

65.   BA-MA: 15 365.7, Treustedt note, 8 October 1941, and 342nd Ia, nr. 13/41g, 8 October 1941; 17 729.9, Anlagen 12 and 17, Pemsel to Turner, 25 and 27 September 1941 (NOKW-183 and 193).

66.   Jewish History Museum, Belgrade, 24-3-1/6-1 (testimony of Milorad Jelesic), 20 February 1945. Jelesic estimated a total of 1,200 victims at Zasavica, which is probably too high. The Sipo-SD report of 9 October 1941 stated that 2,100 "Jews and gypsies" were being executed by the Wehrmacht—805 from Sabac and the rest from Belgrade (NO-3156). M. Jovanovic states that 1,107 refugee Jews were interned at Sabac in June 1941 and 63 local Jews were added in August. She lists 1,057 by name (about 60% male). The report of the *Kreiskommandanturen* 838 of 10 November 1941 noted that of the more than 1,000 Jews in the Sabac camp, only several hundred women remained after the men had been taken away. (Vojno Istoriski Institut, Belgrade, Prague microfilm, roll 8, frame 600.) Turner reported to Böhme that prior to October 18, some 1,000 had already been shot from the Sabac camp.

(BA-MA, 17 729.9, Anlage 100, Turner to Böhme, 25 October 1941, NOKW-561.) On 20 October, the 10-day report of Böhme to List noted that 1,041 hostages had been shot in Belgrade, but it is not clear if this includes the executions of October 9. (BA-MA, 17 729.4, Anlage 159.) In a private letter to Richard Hildebrandt on October 17, Turner noted that in the past eight days he had had 2,000 Jews and 200 gypsies shot. (NO-5810) Thus the exact number of Jews shot in Šabac and Belgrade respectively is unclear, though there is no reason to doubt a total of from 2,100 to 2,200 victims.

67. BA-MA, 17 729.8, entry of 16 October 1941.

68. BA-MA, 17 729.8, Anlage 70, Pemsel order of 19 October 1941 (NOKW-560).

69. NO-5810.

70. For the Rademacher-Suhr visit, see Browning, *Final Solution,* pp. 59–62.

71. Eichmann, when contacted, had simply proposed shooting, and Luther felt that if the Jews in Serbia were a problem, the "military commander must take care of the immediate elimination" of these Jews, for "other military commanders have dealt with considerably greater numbers without even mentioning it." *Ibid.,* pp. 58–59.

72. Apparently the participants of the meeting were made aware of at least some aspects of the European-wide Final Solution then being developed in Berlin, for Rademacher also reported that the Jewish women and children would subsequently be shipped to a "reception camp" *(Auffanglager)* in the east "as soon as the technical possibility exists within the framework of the total solution to the Jewish question." *(Sobald dann im Rahmen der Gesamtlösung der Judenfrage die technische Möglichkeit besteht)* Turner for one seemed immediately to catch the significance of the new policy and especially the potential danger to his career of his past "softness" on the Jewish question. While previously he had worked rather covertly to obtain the deportation of the Serbian Jews, henceforth his reports to Berlin would exaggerate his own role in their destruction. See Turner reports of 3 December 1941 and 15 December 1941 (BA, NS 19/1730) and his letter to Karl Wolff of 11 April 1942 (Berlin Document Center, Turner file).

73. BA-MA, RH 26-117/3, entries of 15–17 October 1941.

74. BA-MA, RH 26-104/13, König report of 20 September 1941.

75. BA-MA: RH 26-104/16, Anlage 486c, König report of 27 October 1941 (NOKW-904); and RW 40.12, Bischofshausen report of 20 October 1941 (NOKW-387).

76. BA-MA, 17 729.9, Anlagen 80 and 81, Faulmüller to IR 749, 21 October 1941, and Pemsel to 65th corps, 22 October 1941.

77. BA-MA, 17 729.2, entry of 22 October 1941.

78. BA-MA, RH 26-104/15, Anlage 53, Bader order of 24 October 1941.

79. BA-MA: 17 729.8, entries of 23 and 24 October 1941; 17 729.9, Anlage 97, Böhme order, nr. 3208/41, 25 October 1941 (NOKW-562).

80. NOKW-802 (Turner to FK, KK, 26 October 1941).

81. BA-MA: RH 26-104/15, Reg. 734 to Div. 704, 28 October 1941 (NOKW-906): RH 26-104/4, entry of 27 October 1941.

82. BA-MA, RW 40.12, Anlage 56, Kogard to Böhme, 29 October 1941.

83. BA-MA, RH 26-104/16, Walther report, 1 November 1941 (NOKW-905). Landgericht Konstanz, 2 Js 823/62, Ermittlungsverfahren gegen Hans-Dietrich Walther, Bd. I, pp. 215–59 (interrogation of Walther). Divisional records credit the first execution with 101 victims, and Walther estimated 200 for each of the last two he presided over. Clearly Turner's subsequent self-aggrandizing claim to Himmler that the Belgrade commandant had refused to use army troops to execute Jews and that he, Turner, had had to have them all shot by the police, is false. BA, NS 19/1730, Turner to Himmler, 15 February 1942. Turner's exaggerated claim was motivated by the transfer of the 64th Reserve Police Battalion to the incoming Higher SS and Police Leader Meyszner, which Turner sought to forestall.

84. BA-MA: 17 729.4, Anlagen 166, 230 and 271; RW 40/13, Anlagen 14 and 26, 40411/2, entry of 9 December 1941; and 14 749/18, Anlage 3 (NOKW-660).

85. BA-MA: 17 729.2, entry of 25 October 1941; 17 729.4, Anlage 202, 10-day report of 30 October 1941 (NOKW-199); RW 40/14, 10-day report of 10 December 1941 (NOKW-660).

86. BA-MA: 15 365.8, 342nd division 10-day report of 30 October 1941; and 15 365.9, 342nd division report of 15 November 1941. In mid-November the "butcher" of Kraljevo and Kragujevac, Major General Hoffmann, was promoted to command of the frontline 342nd, and the more restrained Lt. Gen. Dr. Hinghofer was demoted to the inferior 717th. Böhme charged that Hinghofer's leadership was *"nicht so straff"* as necessary; apparently Hoffmann's own record was viewed quite positively in this regard. BA-MA, 15 365.9, Hinghofer to Böhme, 14 November 1941.

87. See 10-day reports of 10, 20, and 30 November and 10, 20, and 30 December 1941 in: BA-MA, 17 729.4, Anlagen 253, 288 and 329, and RW 40/14, Anlagen 12, 26, and 44.

88. BA-MA, RW 40/23, Aktennotiz of 20 December 1941 (NOKW-474). The report shows that 68% of reprisal shootings had been carried out by the army and 32% by Turner's Militärverwaltung, i.e., the Sipo-SD *Einsatzgruppe* and the 64th Reserve Police Battalion.

89. BA-MA, RW 40/14, Anlage 29, Bader to Verwaltungsstab, 22 December 1941.

90. BA-MA, RW 40/14, Anlage 26, Supplement Nr. 3 to 10-day report of 20 December 1941 (NOKW-840).

3. THE DEVELOPMENT AND PRODUCTION OF THE NAZI GAS VAN

1. Uwe Adam, *Judenpolitik im Dritten Reich* (Düsseldorf, 1972), pp. 303–16; Martin Broszat, "Hitler und die Genesis der 'Endlösung.' Aus Anlass des Thesen von David Irving," *Vierteljahrshefte für Zeitgeschichte* 25 (1977), pp. 748–59; Christopher R. Browning, "Zur Genesis der 'Endlösung.' Eine Antwort an Martin Broszat," *Vierteljahrshefte für Zeitgeschichte* 29 (1981), pp. 97–109; Hans-Heinrich Wilhelm, "Die Einsatzgruppe A der Sicherheitspolizei und des SD 1941/42—Eine exemplarische Studie," *Die Truppe des Weltanschauungskrieges* (Stuttgart, 1981), pp. 622–36.

2. Ernst Klee, *"Euthanasie" im NS-Staat. Die "Vernichtung lebensunwerten Leben."* (Frankfurt/M., 1983); Lothar Gruchmann, "Euthanasie und Justiz im Dritten Reich," *Vierteljahrshefte für Zeitgeschichte* 20 (1972), pp. 234–78; Klaus Dörner, "Nationalsozialismus und Lebensvernichtung," *Vierteljahrshefte für Zeitgeschichte* 15 (1967), pp. 121–52.

3. Adalbert Rückerl, *NS-Vernichtungslager im Spiegel deutscher Strafprozesse: Belzec, Sobibor, Treblinka, Chelmno* (Munich, 1977); Gitta Sereny, *Into That Darkness* (London, 1974).

4. Zentrale Stelle der Landesjustizverwaltungen Ludwigsburg (hereafter cited as ZStL): VI 439 AR-Z 18a/60 (Urteil in die Strafsache gegen Albert Widmann, Landgericht Stuttgart, Ks 19/62), pp. 1–2; 439 AR-Z 18a/1960, vol. I, p. 30 (Ermittlungsverfahren gegen Dr. August Becker, StA Stuttgart 13 Js 328/60, testimony of Hans H.). Berlin Document Center (hereafter cited as BDC): Heess and Widmann SS files. Another notorious "graduate" of the Stuttgart police who became involved in euthanasia and the Final Solution was of course Christian Wirth, the first commandant at Belzec and subsequently Inspector of the three death camps of Operation Reinhard.

5. BDC, Becker SS file. ZStL, 439 AR-Z 18a/1960, vol. III (Anklage gegen Widmann und Becker).

6. ZStL, 439 AR-Z 18a/1960, vol. I, p. 131 (Anzeige gegen Becker und Widmann) and pp. 198–208 (testimony of August Becker).

7. Herbert Lange was born in 1909, entered the NSDAP in May 1932 and the SS in

March 1933, and received officer rank in the SD in 1938. Like many young recruits to the SS, Lange had studied law for eight semesters at the university level and listed his profession as *Jurist*. BDC: Lange SS and RuSHA files; Gunnar C. Boehnert, "The Jurists in the SS-Führer Korps, 1925-1939," *Der Führerstaat: Mythos und Realität*, ed. by Gerhard Hirschfeld and Lothar Kettenacker (Stuttgart, 1981), pp. 361-74.

8. ZStL, 203 AR-Z 69/59, pp. 181-91 (Anklage gegen Wilhelm Koppe, StA Bonn, 8 Js 52/60). Landgericht Hannover, 2 Ks 2/65, Strafverfahren gegen Pradel und Wentritt (hereafter cited as Pradel process), VIII, pp. 71-73 (testimony of Alfred T.), X, p. 245 (Heinrich F.), XII, p. 34 (Alwin G.) and XII, pp. 54-56 (Hans-Hermann R.). There was some confusion among the witnesses as to whether the killing was done exclusively by bottled gas or also by exhaust gas. However, even the witnesses alleging exhaust gas described the gassing process as being controlled from within the driver's cab, and thus Widmann's firm assertion that only bottled gas was used at this time must be correct. According to testimony in a trial concerning the Bornhagen ghetto/labor camp in the Warthegau, a gas van using bottled gas was employed to kill seven hundred Jewish children, elderly, and sick in late November and early December 1941, just when Lange was beginning operations at Chelmno with the new vans using exhaust gas, which likewise indicates that gas vans using exhaust gas were not in use earlier. *Justiz und NS-Verbrechen. Sammlung Deutscher Strafurteile wegen National-sozialistischen Tötungsverbrechen 1945-1966*, VII (Amsterdam, 1971), pp. 229-31 (LG Stuttgart 3 Ks 31/49).

9. Bundesarchiv Koblenz (hereafter cited as BA), NS 19/2576: Koppe to Rediess, 18 October 1940; Rediess to Wolff, 7 November 1940; and Koppe to Wolff, 22 February 1941.

10. Wilhelm, *Die Truppe des Weltanschauungskrieges*, pp. 543, 549-50. Raul Hilberg, *The Destruction of the European Jews* (Chicago, 1961), p. 218. Pradel process, II, pp. 95-102 (ZStL to StA Hannover, 29 March 1960); VIII, pp. 224-25 (testimony of Walter S.); XI, pp. 127-28 (Albert Widmann); and XIV, p. 120 (Helmut H.). ZStL, 439 AR-Z 18a/60, vol. I, pp. 79-90 (testimony of Albert Widmann).

11. BDC: Rauff SS and RuSHA files. Pradel process, XII, pp. 153-61 (testimony of Walter Rauff). Rauff successfully escaped to South America after the war. After a German extradition request for Rauff was rejected by the Chilean government, Rauff granted two interviews in 1964 to German court officials. They took place at the German embassy in Santiago. He died in May 1984.

12. BDC, Pradel SS file. Pradel process, I, pp. 226-29 (testimony of Friedrich Pradel); XV, pp. 100-103, 109 (judgment); Dokumentenbeiheft, 2 (Rauff evaluation of 16 February 1942).

13. BDC, Wentritt SS file. Pradel process, IV, pp. 69-76 (testimony of Harry Wentritt), and XV, pp. 105-6 (judgment).

14. Pradel process, I, pp. 226-29, and V, pp. 261-62 (Pradel testimony). NO-2946 to 2950.

15. Pradel process, V, pp. 251-54, 261-62, and XIV, p. 103 (Pradel testimony). Pradel claimed he protested to Rauff, but was told that any difficulties he made would have to be reported to Heydrich. Rauff denied that he had threatened Pradel; the latter was so ambitious, he said, that that was totally unnecessary. Pradel process, XII, pp. 153-61 (Rauff testimony).

16. Pradel process, IV, pp. 69-76; V, pp. 207-9; and VI, pp. 72-75 (Wentritt testimony).

17. Pradel process, V, pp. 251-54 (Pradel testimony).

18. Pradel process, IV, pp. 69-76; VI, pp. 72-75 (Wentritt testimony).

19. Pradel process, IV, pp. 69-76; X, p. 56 (Wentritt testimony); XIV, p. 137 (judgment).

20. Pradel process, VIII, pp. 221-22 (testimony of Helmut H.); IX, p. 16-19; XIV, p. 118 (testimony of Theodor L.).

21. Ibid.

22. BA, R 58/871, Vermerk of Sipo-SD II D 3 a, 23 June 1942.

23. Pradel process, XV, pp. 141–42 (judgment).

24. Pradel process, IV, p. 117; VII, pp. 52–54; VIII, pp. 227–28 (testimony of Gustav L.); VII, pp. 200–202 (testimony of Walter B.); and IX, pp. 193–94 (testimony of Fritz I.). ZStL, V 203 AR-Z 69/59 (judgment in the Kulmhof process, LG Bonn 8 Ks 3/62), pp. 27, 92. According to Artur Eisenach, Lange's trucks were purchased in Leipzig. See "Opera-Reinhard. Mass Extermination of the Jewish Population in Poland," *Polish Western Affairs* III/1 (1962), p. 97.

25. Pradel process: IX, p. 197 (testimony of Erwin M.), pp. 199 (Herbert D.), p. 200 (Hermann R.); and XI, pp. 30–31 (Georg B.), p. 120 (Julius B.).

26. NO-365 (draft of Wetzel to RK Ostland, 25 October 1941). ZStL, 8 AR-Z 252/59 (Belzec process, LG Muenchen I 110 Ks 3/64), vol. V, pp. 974–75 (Kallmeyer testimony).

27. BA, R 58/871, Rauff to KTI, 20.3.42 (initialed by Pradel).

28. BDC, Becker SS file. Pradel process, II, pp. 95–102 (ZStL to StA Hannover, 29 March 1960); III, pp. 13–29 and pp. 64–68 (Becker testimony).

29. BA, R 58/871: Pradel to Rauff, 4 April 1942, with Rauff marginalia: Rauff to Firma Gaubschat, 30 April 1942; Firma Gaubschat to Rauff, 14 May 1942.

30. *Trials of the Major War Criminals before the International Military Tribunal* (Nürnberg, 1947–49) (hereafter cited as IMT), IV, pp. 323, 334 (Ohlendorf testimony), XXVI, pp. 103–5 (501-PS: Becker to Rauff, 15 May 1942). Pradel process, III, 13–29 and 64–68 (Becker testimony).

31. Pradel process, V, pp. 55–58 (testimony of Anton S.).

32. BA, R 58/871, Just to Rauff, 5 June 1942. A facsimilie of this document is printed in Kogon, Langbein, Rückerl, *Nationalsozialistische Massentötungen durch Giftgas*, pp. 333–37.

33. Born in 1899, Just was a front soldier and welder before joining the Schupo in 1920. He was hired by the Gestapo in 1937, joined the SS in 1938, and finally became a party member in 1941. BDC: Just SS file.

34. BA, R 58/871, Just to Rauff, 5 June 1942, with Rauff marginalia, 10 June 1942.

35. BA, R 58/871: Vermerk and Wentritt draft to Firma Gaubschat, 23 June 1942; Firma Gaubschat to Sipo-SD, 20 and 24 September 1942.

36. Rückerl, *NS-Vernichtungslager im Spiegel deutscher Strafprozesse*, pp. 292–93.

37. See Chapter 4.

38. IMT, XXVI, p. 108 (501-PS, Befh. Sipo-SD Ostland to RSHA, 6.15.42). Pradel process, III, pp. 64–68 (Becker testimony). More than fifteen thousand German and Austrian Jews were deported to Minsk in sixteen transports between May and October 1942. Most were immediately killed at Trostinez by gas vans and mass shooting. Because of the cleaning problem and other defects in the gas vans, however, shooting was the primary killing method. *Justiz und NS-Verbrechen*, XIX (Amsterdam, 1978), pp. 193–95 (LG Koblenz 9 Ks 2/62). For other employment of the gas van see Kogon, Langbein, Rückerl, *Nationalsozialistische Massentötungen durch Gift gas*, pp. 87–109.

4. THE SEMLIN GAS VAN AND THE FINAL SOLUTION IN SERBIA

1. Bundesarchiv-Militärarchiv Freiburg (hereafter cited as BA-MA), RW 40/79: Schröder memorandum, 17 July 1941, and Turner memorandum, 27 August 1941. See also Helmut Krausnick, "Die Einsatzgruppen vom Anschluss Österreichs bis zum Feldzug gegen die Sowjetunion. Entwicklung und Verhältnis zur Wehrmacht," Part I of *Die Truppe des Weltanschauungskrieges* (Stuttgart, 1981), p. 137.

2. Vojno Istorijski Institut Belgrade (hereafter cited as V.I.I.), German archive, 27-2-38, telephone book of the Feldnachrichten Kommandantur 32.

3. V.I.I., German archive, Prague microfilm, roll 8/frame 629.

4. V.I.I., German archive, 50-4-2, 50-4-7, 50-8-1, 66-2-3/a, and 66-2-31.

5. NI-1575, summary report of Gurski, 23 March 1945.

6. *Akten zur Deutschen Aussenpolitik, 1918–1945*, (hereafter cited as ADAP) Series D, Part 2 (Göttingen, 1970), pp. 475–76.

7. See especially the "Verordnung betreffend die Juden und Zigeuner" of 30 May 1941. Copy in the Jevrejski Istorijski Muzej Belgrade (hereafter cited as J.I.M.), 21-1-1/20.

8. Zdenko Löwenthal, ed., *The Crimes of the Fascist Occupants and Their Collaborators Against Jews in Yugoslavia* (Belgrade, 1957), pp. 2–3.

9. Christopher R. Browning, *The Final Solution and the German Foreign Office* (New York, 1978), pp. 56–62.

10. BA-MA, 17 729.8: Entries for 26 and 30 September, 6 and 28 October 1941. (NOKW-193 and NOKW-262)

11. Politisches Archiv des Auswärtigen Amtes Bonn (hereafter cited as PA), Gesandschaft Belgrad 62/6: Benzler to Agram, 29 October 1941, and Troll to Belgrade, 11 November 1941.

12. NOKW-801, Turner to Feld- und Kreiskommandanturen, 11 November 1941.

13. Bundesarchiv Koblenz (hereafter cited as BA), R 26 VI/GWS-476, correspondence of 16 December 1941.

14. NI-1575, summary report of Gurski, 23 March 1945.

15. Löwenthal, *The Crimes of the Fascist Occupants*, p. 4.

16. J.I.M., 24-2-2/4, testimony of Dr. Lev Brandeis. Landgericht Köln, 24 Ks 1/52 and 2/53, Strafverfahren gegen Emanuel Schäfer (hereafter cited as Schäfer process), II, pp. 730–41 (testimony of Hedvig Schönfein). Landgericht Dortmund, 45 Ks 2/68, Strafverfahren gegen Herbert Andorfer (hereafter cited as Andorfer process), II, pp. 8–11 (testimony of Herbert Andorfer). Institut für Zeitgeschichte (hereafter cited as IfZ), Eichmann document 1432 (report of Milan Markovic).

17. NOKW-1150, memorandum of Major Jais, 5 December 1941.

18. NOKW-610, 10-day report of the plenipotentiary command general in Serbia, 20 December 1941.

19. V.I.I., Nedic archiv, 36-33/8-2, bill for feeding the *Judenlager.*

20. NOKW-1221, 10-day report, 10 March 1942.

21. NOKW-1077, daily report, 19 March 1942.

22. Andorfer process, II, p. 42.

23. Löwenthal, *The Crimes of the Fascist Occupants*, p. 4. IfZ, Eichmann document 1119 (report of A. Alexander).

24. V.I.I., Nedic archive, 26-14/7-1, Belgrade municipal government to department of social welfare, 15 December 1941.

25. V.I.I., Nedic archive, 26-22/1-1 and 3, Enge to Belgrade municipal government, 31 December 1941, and Belgrade municipal government to commandant of the *Judenlager,* 1 January 1942.

26. V.I.I., Nedic archive, 36-22/11-1, Enge to Belgrade municipal government, 1 January 1942.

27. V.I.I., Nedic archive: 36-25/1-3, Enge report of 16 January 1942; 36-27/1-2, Enge to Belgrade municipal government, 20 January 1942.

28. V.I.I., Nedic archive, 36-30/1-5, Andorfer to Belgrade municipal government, 1 February 1942.

29. V.I.I., Nedic archive, document number unclear, Belgrade municipal government to department of social welfare, 3 February 1942.

30. BA, R 26 VI/GWS-476: Jovanovic to Turner, 24 February 1942; and Turner to Neuhausen, 16 March 1942.

31. BA, R 26 VI/GWS-476: Jovanovic to Turner, 20 April 1942; and Ranze to Turner, 6 July 1942.

32. Berlin Document Center (hereafter cited as BDC), August Meyszner SS-file.

33. BDC, Schäfer SS-file. Schaefer process, II, pp. 185–91.

34. Schäfer process, III, p. 627.

35. BDC, Schäfer SS-file.

36. IfZ, Zs 573.

37. Krausnick, *Die Truppe des Weltanschauungskrieges*, p. 47.

38. H. G. Adler, *Der Verwaltete Mensch: Studien zur Deportation der Juden aus Deutschland* (Tübingen, 1974), pp. 129–33; Seev Goschen, "Eichmann und die Nisko-Aktion im Oktober 1939," *Vierteljahrshefte für Zeitgeschichte* 29/1 (1981), pp. 74–96. This renders preposterous Schäfer's subsequent claim that he was accused by the Higher SS and Police Leader Erich von dem Bach-Zelewski of making Upper Silesia an "El Dorado" for Jews and Poles and was therefore demoted to the Köln *Staatspolizeistelle* with a much smaller staff (100 instead of 400 personnel). Von dem Bach-Zelwski denied any role in Schäfer's transfer and offered the more plausible explanation that it might have resulted from the fact that the Silesian *Gauleiter* Joseph Wagner, a protégé of Göring, was staffing "his" newly incorporated territories with his own men, while Schäfer was clearly a Heydrich loyalist. Schäfer process, I, pp. 190–93, and II, pp. 266–67.

39. *Justiz und NS-Verbrechen: Sammlung deutscher Strafurteile wegen Nationalsozialistischer Tötungsverbrechen 1945–1966* (Amsterdam, 1974), XII, p. 575. This trial, 24 Ks 3/53 of the Landgericht Köln, followed shortly after Schäfer's trial for crimes in Serbia and involved other defendants as well.

40. Schäfer process, II, pp. 191 and 331.

41. Schäfer process, II, p. 357 (testimony of Walter U.); III, p. 585 (testimony of Paul Bader); and II, p. 351 (testimony of Dr. Joerg-Wilhelm H.).

42. *Justiz und NS-Verbrechen*, XII, p. 595. Schäfer process, I, p. 90 (judgment of the Bielefeld denazification proceedings).

43. Schäfer process, II, pp. 206–8 (testimony of Marianne K.), pp. 247–49 (Ernst M.), and p. 306 (Hans S.).

44. Schäfer process: II, pp. 348–49 (testimony of Walter H.); p. 356 (August K.); and III, pp. 654–58 (Bruno M.).

45. Schäfer process, II, pp. 194–98.

46. BDC, Sattler SS-file.

47. V.I.I., German archive, 32-12-3 (testimony of Toma Pfeffer).

48. BDC, Andorfer SS-file. Andorfer process, II, pp. 8–9, 42, and III, p. 305.

49. Landgericht Stuttgart, Ks 21/67, Strafverfahren gegen Edgar Enge (hereafter cited as Enge process); Haftheft, pp. 45–51; Hauptakten, pp. 44–47, 183. Andorfer process, I, p. 87.

50. The Berlin Document Center contains no SS-officer file for Edgar Enge.

51. NOKW-497, Liepe report, 13 October 1941. Enge process, Haftheft, p. 55.

52. BDC, Turner SS-file, Turner to Wolff, 11 April 1942.

53. BA, NS 19/1730: Turner's monthly political report of 3 December 1941, and Turner's Gesamtsituationsbericht to the Reichsführer-SS, 15 February 1942.

54. For example, in his report of 15 February 1942, Turner claims that the Belgrade

garrison refused to shoot Jews, and "exclusively" on his orders the *Einsatzgruppe* and police then under his command shot all the male Jews and gypsies in Belgrade and removed the women and children. In fact, the first order to shoot Jews came from General Franz Böhme to Turner (NOKW-192 of 4 October 1941); these executions were carried out mostly by military troops (army records credit Turner's men with shooting 3616 of the 11,164 recorded hostage shootings—roughly one-third—though army statistics did not include the army shootings of Jews in Sabac (NOKW-474, Aktennotiz of 20 December 1941); the Belgrade garrison was among the troops carrying out mass executions of Jews (NOKW-905, Walther report of 4 November 1941), and Turner himself briefly delayed turning over Jews to army firing squads (ADAP, XIII, Part 2, pp. 570–72, Rademacher report on his trip to Belgrade, 25 October 1941); and Browning, *The Final Solution and the German Foreign Office*, pp. 56–67).

55. Schäfer process, II, pp. 199–204, 331–34, 342–44. Landgericht Hannover, 2 Ks 2/65, Strafverfahren gegen Pradel und Wentritt (hereafter cited as Pradel process), VIII, pp. 55–57, and XII, pp. 238–39.

56. ADAP, XIII, Part 2, pp. 570–72 and 805 (Luther Vermerk of December 9, 1941).

57. Pradel process, VII, pp. 55–57, and XII, pp. 238–39. Enge process, Hauptakten, p. 35.

58. Werner Präg and Wolfgang Jacobmeyer, ed., *Das Diensttagebuch des deutschen Generalgouverneurs in Polen 1939–1945* (Stuttgart, 1975), p. 457.

59. Martin Broszat, "Hitler und die Genesis der 'Endlösung'. Aus Anlass der Thesen von David Irving," *Vierteljahrshefte für Zeitgeschichte* 25 (1977), pp. 739–75. The English version of Broszat's article is found in *Yad Vashem Studies*, XIII (1979), pp. 73–125. For my critique of Broszat's thesis, see "Zur Genesis der 'Endlösung'. Eine Antwort an Martin Broszat," *Vierteljahrshefte für Zeitgeschichte* 27/ (1981)1, pp. 97–109.

60. Schäfer process: II, pp. 331–374; III, pp. 624 and 690.

61. For Andorfer's account, see Andorfer process, II, pp. 12–16, 41–46, and III, 3–31; Enge process, Hauptakten, pp. 83–88, 99–103, 162–63.

62. All attempts to trace the drivers, Götz and Meyer, have been unsuccessful. The few gas-van drivers who have been identified were full-time Sipo-SD drivers subsequently assigned to gas-van duty. Pradel process, XV, pp. 49–56. If the RSHA could draw upon its own chemists and mechanics, it is not surprising it should draw upon its own pool of experienced drivers. With over 4,000 vehicles, there could have been no shortage.

63. Schäfer process, III, pp. 727–41 (Schönfein testimony).

64. For the testimony of Karl W., see Pradel process, XII, pp. 223–32, and XIV, p. 125; Enge process, Hauptakten, pp. 104–7; and Andorfer process, I, pp. 149–152, and III, pp 43–48. For the testimony of Leo L., see Pradel process, XIII, p 47–50; Enge process, Hauptakten, pp. 3–6, 25–30; and Andorfer process, I, pp. 153–54, and III, pp. 48–51.

65. "However odd it may sound, I would also like to mention here, that no presents or rewards were given to the participants in this action by the leadership." (So komisch es klingen mag, möchte ich auch hier erwähnen, dass seitens der Führung keinerlei Geschencke oder Belohnung an die an dieser Aktion Beteiligten stattgefunden hat.) For Enge's account, see Enge process, Haftheft, pp. 56–62, and Hauptakten, pp. 183–86; Andorfer process, III, pp. 55–61.

66. Pradel process, XII, pp. 7–8; and Andorfer process, I, p. 154.

67. Schönfein, the Swiss Protestant wife of a Jewish doctor, testified that 100 per trip was regular. Karl W. and Leo L. initially estimated 100 per truck, but subsequently reduced that to 50. At eight trips per week for nine weeks, it would have required an average load of 87 to gas 6,280 persons.

68. Schönfein confirms that Andorfer was in camp on the last morning. Leo L. gives the

only consistent and believable testimony on the shooting of the Serbian prisoners. He had returned from his position guarding the entrance when Enge announced to the prisoners that they were to be shot. He then returned to his post and heard machine-pistol fire from more than one gun. Not surprisingly, the testimony of Enge and Karl W. is inconsistent, implausible, and hopelessly self-serving on this incident.

69. *Trials of the Major War Criminals before the International Military Tribunal* (Nürnberg, 1947–1949), XXVI, p. 109 (501-PS, Schäfer to Pradel, 8 June 1942).

70. Andorfer process, I, p. 60 (testimony of Kurt S.).

71. NOKW-1421, Felber to Meyszner, 24 December 1943.

72. IfZ, Eichmann document 1119 (report of A. Alexander).

73. PA, Pol. IV(348), Rademacher memorandum, 29 May 1942.

74. NOKW-926, report on the trip of the Military Commander Southeast to Serbia, 7–14 June 1942.

75. Pradel process, XIV, p. 127 (Enge testimony).

76. Enge process, Hauptakten, p. 58; and Andorfer process, III, p. 58 (Enge testimony).

77. Pradel process, XII, p. 8 (Karl W. testimony); and Andorfer process, I, p. 59 (testimony of Kurt S.).

78. Andorfer process, III, p. 42; Schäfer process: II, p. 416; III, p. 497 (Fritz M. testimony) and p. 598 (Ernst W. testimony); II, p. 353 (Dr. R. testimony).

79. Pradel process, I, p. 213 (testimony of Dr. Walter U.).

80. Schäfer process, III, pp. 647, 654–58 (testimony of Bruno M.).

81. Landgericht Kassel, 3 Js 11/66, Ermittlungsverfahren gegen Walter Liepe, p. 30 (testimony of Karl B.) and p. 44 (testimony of Anton S.).

82. J.I.M., 24-2-2/4 (testimony of Dr. Lev Brandeis); Schäfer process, II, pp. 387–88; and Pradel process, I, p. 210 (testimony of Alexander F.).

83. Nürnberg Staatsarchiv, Rep. 502 VI, T 4 (affidavit of Wilhelm Gustav Temple).

84. Andorfer process, III, pp. 3–31, 67–70 (Andorfer's court testimony). On compartmentalization and routinization, see also George Kren and Leon Rappoport, *The Holocaust and the Crisis of Human Behavior* (New York, 1980), pp. 140–41.

85. Schäfer process, I, p. 26 (testimony of Frederick K.), and II, p. 353 (testimony of Dr. R.).

CONCLUSION

1. While recent studies of German attitudes to the Nazi persecution of the Jews differ in their speculation over how much most people actually knew of the mass murders and the degree of "opposition" or "dissent," they are uniform in their conclusions that the bulk of the German population was shockingly apathetic and indifferent toward the ultimate fate of the Jews in the war years. If most Germans were not fanatical or "paranoid" anti-Semites, they were "mild," "latent," or passive anti-Semites, for whom the Jews had become a "depersonalized," abstract, and alien entity beyond human empathy and the "Jewish Question" a legitimate subject of state policy deserving solution. As we have seen in the case of the Wehrmacht in Serbia, such widespread attitudes were more than sufficient in wartime for Germans to accept the identification of the Jews with the enemy and hence to facilitate not only their acquiescence but also their active participation and even initiative in mass murder. Ian Kershaw, *Popular Opinion and Political Dissent in the Third Reich:* Bavaria 1933–1945 (Oxford, 1983), and "The Persecution of the Jews and German Popular Opinion in the Third Reich," *Leo Baeck Institute Yearbook* 26 (1981), 261–89; Sarah Gordon, *Hitler, Germans;*

and the "Jewish Question" (Princeton, 1984); Otto Dov Kulka, " 'Public Opinion' in Nazi Germany: The Final Solution," *The Jerusalem Quarterly* 26 (Winter 1982), 34–45. Also of interest in this regard are Hans-Heinrich Wilhelm, "Wie geheim war die Endlösung," *Miscellanea,* ed. by Wolfgang Benz (Stuttgart, 1980), pp. 131–48; Marlis Steinert, *Hitler's War and the Germans* (Athens, Ohio, 1977); and Lawrence Stokes, "The German People and the Destruction of the European Jews," *Central European History* 6 (1973), 167–91.

Index

ABOUT THE AUTHOR

Christopher R. Browning is an Associate Professor of History at Pacific Lutheran University. His publications include *The Final Solution and the German Foreign Office,* also available from Holmes & Meier.